Julius Caesar

An Enthralling Guide to the Conquest, Power, and Assassination of Rome's Eternal Dictator

Free limited time bonus

Stop for a moment. We have a free bonus set up for you. The problem is this: we forget 90% of everything that we read after 7 days. Crazy fact, right? Here's the solution: we've created a printable, 1-page pdf summary for this book that you're reading now. All you have to do to get your free pdf summary is to go to the following website:

https://livetolearn.lpages.co/enthrallinghistory/

Or, Scan the QR code!

Once you do, it will be intuitive. Enjoy, and thank you!

Table of Contents

Introduction

This book is the history of the astonishing life and times of Julius Caesar. It is filled with battles, sieges, conspiracies, and assassinations. The work is perfect for beginners and even those knowledgeable about the topic. It presents Caesar in a new way so modern people can understand the Roman world through themes that are relevant today, such as democracy and authoritarianism.

Explore the remarkable personality of Caesar and his scandalous life. Learn about his political maneuvering and his great affair with Cleopatra. See how Roman culture and society shaped him into the man he became.

Discover Caesar's greatest battles, and learn about his strategic genius. You will see how Caesar came to be regarded as one of the greatest generals of all time. After all, he conquered much of western Europe and beat foreign and Roman enemies.

This work does not gloss over the darker side of Caesar either. It talks about his many crimes, such as the massacres of Germanic tribes. This work presents one of history's greatest generals as his contemporaries would have seen him.

Such a remarkable man has had a tremendous impact. You will learn how Caesar, through his many and varied conquests, laid the foundation for Europe and paved the way for the zenith of Roman power. It also shows how he was a master of propaganda and how he inspired dictators and authoritarian figures, even in the modern day.

Chapter 1: The Young Julius Caesar

The Early Years of the Future Conqueror

Julius Caesar was born into an aristocratic, or patrician, Roman family. There is no agreement on Caesar's birthday, but most believe it was July 12th, 100 BCE. His family was a member of the prestigious clan of *gens Julia*, which had an illustrious history. They claimed to have immigrated to Rome many centuries prior and originated in the fabled city of Alba Longa, which a Roman king once destroyed. The Julii also claimed descent from Julus, a son of the Trojan hero Aeneas, one of the most important figures in Roman mythology. This dubious claim meant the clan descended from a great hero and had divine origins. Aeneas was the son of the Roman goddess of love, Venus. The pedigree of the Julii was well known and added to their prestige.

As one of the old patrician families, they could claim to be members of the original aristocracy. They were distinct from the plebeian families, which had only fully integrated into the Roman aristocracy by Caesar's time. The patrician and plebeian split in the aristocracy contributed to the rivalry between the populares and the optimates factions, which dominated politics in Rome. In traditional societies such as Rome, an ancient pedigree added to a family's prestige and often translated into political influence and the ability to win elections for major magistracies, such as that of consul (one of the highest elected public offices in the Roman Republic). Roman Patrician families can be likened to modern-day political families with significant influence.

Only in the 3rd century BCE did the family become politically important. The first consul with the name Caesar was listed in 157 BCE. Two Julii consuls were elected in the 90s BCE, including Caesar's uncle Sextus. Despite this, the family was not considered one of the greatest families, and in the decades before Caesar was born, they had lost some of their prestige and influence. Caesar's father, Gaius Julius Caesar, was a member of the Roman Senate and held the office of praetor in the 90s BCE. Julius's aunt was married to Marius, an important Roman figure who defeated a massive German barbarian invasion in the Cimbrian War (113-101 BCE). He is widely credited with reforming the military and creating the Roman military machine, but some historians reject this idea.

Marius was a "new man" whose family was not originally Roman and had only recently become prominent in the city. As a new man, Marius was sympathetic to the populares party. The populares and optimates were the two dominant factions in Roman politics, though they did not really function like modern political parties. They were more like opposing ideologies held by senators. The optimates, whose name roughly translates as "the best men," represented the conservative senatorial elite. They favored preserving the traditional power of the Senate and resisted efforts to redistribute land or extend political rights more broadly. The populares sought to bypass the Senate by appealing directly to the popular assemblies, the bodies in which ordinary Roman citizens had a voice. They generally supported land reform and greater political inclusion for plebeians and Italian citizens.

The divide was as much about power and self-interest as it was about genuine ideology. Many populares came from aristocratic backgrounds themselves, and their championing of the common people was often a means of outmaneuvering their rivals in the Senate.

Marius's belief in merit was welcomed by ordinary citizens. Politics was a family business in Rome, so Julius Caesar's future political sympathies often lay with the populares. This was not as strange as it appears. The Julii had lost status and wealth, and by associating with the "new men," they hoped to regain lost ground. They could not afford to be conservative and snobbish, given their waning influence and potential financial difficulties. The wealthy patrician families would not fully accept them because of their relative lack of wealth. Moreover, like many influential families, they believed that the populares had the best interests of Rome at heart, unlike the optimates, who only wanted more land and power.

We know little about Caesar's childhood. It can be safely assumed that he was given a traditional upbringing and education. His mother, Aurelia, was a member of the powerful Cotta family and molded her son's character while providing him with support. Despite coming from a privileged background, his upbringing sought to toughen him both physically and mentally. The aim of his education was to enable him to succeed in Rome's competitive world and advance his family's interests. He would have been educated by enslaved or freed tutors and taught Latin, Greek, and rhetoric. Later in life, he was considered very cultured and even wrote verses. As a teenager, he would have studied Roman law and oratory, or the art of persuasion. He excelled at the latter, as he was considered to be a great orator, which was a factor in his political success.

Like every other aristocratic male Roman, the young Julius Caesar was expected to enter into a political and military career. At the age of sixteen, he assumed the toga, symbolizing his entry into manhood and assuming his civic responsibilities. As a young aristocrat, he was expected to advance the interests of his formerly illustrious family. In the Julii household, the masks of his dead relatives were hung. He would have seen the busts of his ancestors, such as Aeneas. The young Caesar would have been expected to equal, if not surpass, their feats. This need for recognition and respect was what drove him during his life.

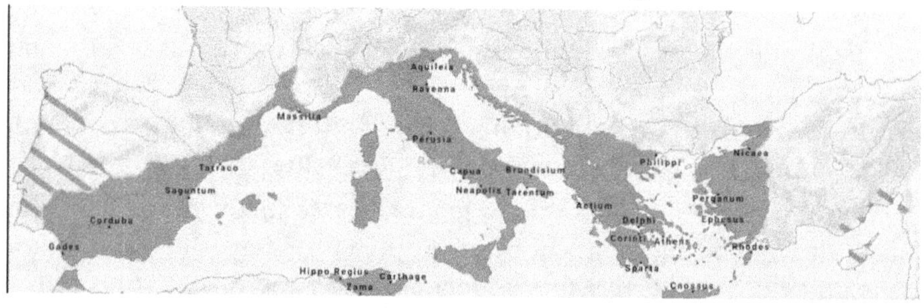

The Roman Republic's extent around 100 BCE. ('

The origin of the name Caesar is itself a matter of some debate. The most popular explanation, and the one that has endured into modern times, is that it derived from the Latin word for a surgical birth. According to this tradition, an ancestor of Julius was delivered by what we now call a caesarean section, and the family took its name from it. This is almost certainly a myth. In the ancient world, caesarean sections were only performed when the mother was already dead or dying, as the procedure was fatal for her. Since Caesar's mother, Aurelia, not only survived his birth but lived long enough to play a significant role in his upbringing, this explanation does not hold up in the case of Julius.

Other theories have been proposed over the centuries. Some ancient writers suggested the name derived from a Punic word for elephant, after an ancestor supposedly killed one in battle. Others connected it to a word meaning a thick head of hair, which would be somewhat ironic given Caesar's well-documented sensitivity about his own baldness in later life. Unfortunately, the true origin of the name is lost to history.

Dangerous Times

The best way for young aristocrats to achieve their ambitions was through public service and following the *cursus honorum*, which involved securing high offices after demonstrating their ability. Caesar was an ardent admirer of his uncle Marius and looked to him as a role model in many ways. Based on his later career, it seems that Caesar learned from Marius that real power lay in the military and that old traditions could be easily set aside. He also learned from him that any successful politician needed the public's support.

Julius was also inspired by Alexander the Great and wanted to be a conqueror from his early years. Later writers believed that Alexander had inspired him to become the ruler of Rome. However, this is unlikely, as Caesar would have learned, as part of his education, that kings were not acceptable to the freedom-loving Romans.

Perhaps Caesar's greatest motivation was his desire for *dignitas*, honor and widespread respect. Throughout his career, his obsession was to earn more and more glory to enhance his dignitas. For Caesar, dignitas meant having a good reputation, which would ensure that his name would live forever. He was eager to secure more power, which ultimately led him to become the dictator of Rome.

The sources are fragmentary, but he possibly became engaged to or even married a young lady called Cossutia, the daughter of a wealthy equestrian (the property-owning class below the senatorial class), at the age of sixteen. This was not a love match but a practical arrangement between two families. If the two did marry, Caesar later left her to marry another. His union with Cossutia produced no children.

Young Caesar entered public life at a perilous time. The Roman Republic, in the aftermath of the Second Punic War, had secured a

Mediterranean empire. Its lands stretched from Spain across the central Mediterranean into Greece and western Asia Minor and also included territories in North Africa. The Roman Republic had become prosperous, but inequality, competition among the aristocrats, and corruption led to social unrest and divisions. Increasingly, the aristocrats, or optimates, were expanding their landholdings at the expense of small citizen farmers, making land reform a subject of controversy. The optimates had twice defeated an attempt at land reform by the Gracchi brothers in the late 2nd century BCE.

The rapid expansion of the Republic after the defeat of the Carthaginians placed tremendous strain on the government and bureaucracy. Rome's government and constitution had been designed for a city-state, not a large empire. Without oversight, many governors acted like monarchs and became notorious for corruption. Increasingly, the legions owed their allegiance to their military commanders rather than to Rome. Moreover, after the Social War (91–88 BCE), a war fought between Rome and its autonomous allies in Italy, many Italians became citizens, upsetting the balance between plebeians and patricians and leading to intense political infighting. In addition, the wealth of the provinces was used by politicians to secure support, making politics even more competitive and bloody.

Civil War and Political Violence

In 84 BCE, Lucius Cornelius Cinna was serving his fourth consecutive consulship, having dominated Roman politics since 87. Around this time, Caesar's father, Gaius Julius Caesar, died (probably in 85 or 84 BCE). He had been a praetor and later governed the province of Asia. His death left the teenage Julius as head of his household.

To most Romans, Caesar would have still seemed a young man with limited immediate prospects. The Julii were an ancient patrician family, but they were not among the most dominant political houses of the period and had not produced a consul in decades. Even so, Caesar had important connections. Gaius Marius, one of the most famous generals of his day, was his uncle by marriage, having married Caesar's aunt Julia. These ties mattered. Roman politics ran on wealth, reputation, and networks of obligation. Patronage shaped elections and careers. Later in life, Caesar would build vast patronage networks of his own.

For someone who would become one of Rome's greatest generals, Caesar first entered public life not as a soldier but as a priest. In the 80s

BCE, he was appointed to the priesthood of Jupiter, the Flamen Dialis. The position came with heavy religious taboos and restrictions. For instance, the Flamen Dialis could not leave Italy, could not ride a horse, and was effectively barred from military command. These were serious limits in a society that rewarded ambition and battlefield success. However, Caesar did not hold the office for long, as the civil war soon disrupted the arrangement.

Soon after earning this position, the young Caesar married Cornelia, the daughter of Cinna. This marriage also would have been more about politics and binding two families together than any true love. By marrying Cinna's daughter, Caesar aligned himself with the ruling faction in Rome. That alignment would later put him in danger.

The 80s BCE were marked by civil war. Marius and Cinna seized control of Rome after driving out their opponents. Populares and optimates competed fiercely for power. Sulla, one of the Roman Republic's most accomplished generals and a leading figure among the conservative aristocracy, was at the time commanding an army at Nola in southern Italy. He had been appointed to lead the war against Mithridates VI of Pontus, whose forces had seized Roman territory in Asia Minor and encouraged revolts across the eastern Mediterranean. In 88 BCE, however, the political struggle in Rome took a dramatic turn. Through the efforts of Marius and his allies, the command against Mithridates was transferred from Sulla to Marius.

Rather than accept the decision, Sulla took an unprecedented step. He ordered his legions to march on Rome itself. No Roman general had ever led a standing army against the city before. This act shattered a long-standing political taboo and showed how deeply military loyalty had begun to shift from the state to individual commanders.

Sulla seized Rome by force, drove his opponents into exile, and reasserted control over the government. Once the situation in the city had temporarily stabilized, he left Italy to lead the Eastern campaign. Sulla confronted Mithridates VI, whose expansion had included the massacre of thousands of Romans and Italians in Asia and the occupation of key Greek cities such as Athens. The war was brutal and destructive, especially in Greece, where several cities were besieged and sacked before Sulla eventually forced Mithridates into a settlement.

While Sulla was away, the Marian regime carried out violent reprisals against its enemies. Political killings were common, and the atmosphere in Rome was tense and unstable. Caesar, who was still very young and connected by marriage to Cinna, was not a central actor in these events.

Marius, who was already seventy years old, soon died. Cinna was later killed in a mutiny by his own soldiers. When Sulla returned from the East, he defeated the remaining opposition and again took Rome by force. Though resistance continued in places like Spain, where Sertorius maintained a rival Marian stronghold, Rome itself fell firmly under Sulla's control.

Danger and Opportunities

Sulla wanted to preserve the old order and punish those who had challenged it. He drew up lists of his political enemies—the infamous proscriptions—condemning hundreds to death and ordering their property

Bust of Julius Caesar as a youth. [2]

seized. A reign of terror began in the city, and men of all ranks died. Historians have likened this period to a counter-revolution.

The newly married Julius was in grave danger. He was Marius's nephew by marriage and Cinna's son-in-law. Sulla ordered him to divorce his wife, Cornelia. Remarkably, the young man refused. As a consequence, Sulla stripped him of his priesthood of Jupiter and confiscated Cornelia's dowry. Caesar went into hiding, moving between places while reportedly suffering from a severe fever. According to ancient sources, his family, fellow priests, and even the Vestal Virgins interceded on his behalf.

Some ancient sources claim Caesar was placed on the proscription lists, though modern historians doubt this. He appears to have been targeted and threatened without being formally condemned, though. Eventually, through the efforts of influential relatives and supporters, Sulla relented. He was not known for his mercy. According to legend, he warned those pleading Caesar's case that the young man would one day prove dangerous, saying there were "many Mariuses" in him.

Caesar left Rome. He was not formally exiled, but the political climate made it the safer choice. He served on the staff of Marcus Minucius Thermus, the governor of the Roman province of Asia. Caesar was sent as a diplomat to the court of Nicomedes IV, the king of Bithynia, to secure naval support. He remained there longer than expected, and his enemies later claimed he had an affair with the king. They referred to Caesar as the "Queen of Bithynia." This was almost certainly political slander. There is no credible evidence to support a relationship between the two, but his prolonged stay certainly gave the rumors room to spread.

Caesar saw his first serious military action at the siege of Mytilene in 81 BCE. Mytilene, the principal city on the island of Lesbos, had supported Rome's enemy Mithridates VI during the First Mithridatic War and had refused to submit to Sulla's terms. Thermus moved to subdue the city, possibly in coordination with the Roman commander Lucius Licinius Lucullus. During the fighting, Caesar saved the lives of fellow soldiers. For his bravery, he was awarded the Civic Crown, one of Rome's highest military honors. It was a remarkable distinction for a young man of nineteen. Holders of the crown had the right to wear it at public occasions, a privilege that added to Caesar's growing public image.

After Mytilene, Caesar served briefly under Publius Servilius Vatia Isauricus in Cilicia, where Roman forces were engaged against pirates and local bandits. In 78 BCE, Sulla died. Caesar could now safely return to Rome. It is worth noting that, however hard the loss of his priesthood was, it had freed him from the strict taboos of the office. The restrictions placed on him with that office would have made a political and military career all but impossible. Whether Caesar would have found another path regardless is impossible to say.

A bust of Sulla.[8]

Captured by Pirates

Rome was now governed by Sulla's constitutional settlement, with his supporters firmly in control. As mentioned, Sulla believed that Rome had become unstable because ambitious politicians were appealing directly to the masses and bypassing the Senate's traditional authority. To prevent this, he strengthened the Senate's control over the government, weakened officials who represented the common people, and introduced stricter rules about how politicians could advance in their careers. His aim was to restore what he saw as the old, orderly system of aristocratic rule.

Caesar began a legal career. He made his name not by winning cases but by daring to prosecute powerful men. He brought charges against Senator Gaius Antonius Hybrida, whom the other senators accused of profiting from Sulla's proscriptions, and against a corrupt governor of Macedonia. Caesar secured no convictions in either case, but the prosecutions earned him a reputation for boldness.

To further his education, Caesar traveled to Rhodes in 75 BCE to study rhetoric and philosophy. On the way, Cilician pirates captured him and demanded a ransom for his release. According to sources, including the famous historian Plutarch, Caesar remained remarkably composed throughout his captivity. He kept to his routines, wrote poetry, and even played dice with his captors. When he learned they had demanded twenty talents for his release, he reportedly told them he was worth fifty. He also promised, apparently in earnest, that he would have them crucified when he was free. They took this as a joke. It was not. After his ransom was paid, he gathered a small force, hunted down his captors, and crucified them. This story spread and added to Caesar's growing reputation in Rome.

Caesar then continued to Rhodes, a renowned center of learning in the Hellenistic world. He improved his oratory and developed a style that contemporaries found persuasive. Some ancient sources suggest he was also exposed to Epicurean ideas during this period, though whether he studied the philosophy in a formal manner is unclear. Epicureanism states that the highest good is the absence of pain and disturbance rather than the pursuit of pleasure in the conventional sense. Some of Caesar's later statements have led historians to speculate that Epicureanism left an impression on him, but we do not know this for sure.

His studies were interrupted by the outbreak of the Third Mithridatic War, commonly dated to 73 to 63 BCE. Rome's long-standing enemy, Mithridates VI of Pontus, again moved to expand his influence in the eastern Mediterranean. Some sources suggest Caesar became involved in the early stages of the war. He appears to have raised a small local force in Asia Minor and used it against forces aligned with Mithridates, though this was not a major action. After a brief period, he returned to Rome. A political career was Caesar's priority, and Rome was where that career would be made.

Chapter 2: Caesar's Rise to Power

Caesar: Priest and Politician

Sulla died in 78 BCE, but his reforms remained in place. His supporters, the optimates, held firm control of the Senate and the major offices of state. The key target of Sulla's reforms had been the tribunate. The tribunate was the office held by the tribunes of the plebs. Each year, several tribunes were elected to represent ordinary Romans and protect them from abuses by powerful nobles. They could propose laws to the people and veto decisions made by other officials, including the Senate. Because tribunes had the power to block government actions, the office became a powerful political weapon. Sulla weakened the tribunate by stripping those tribunes of much of their authority, making it far harder for them to challenge the Senate.

This was the central grievance of those who opposed Sulla's settlement. No one wanted a return to civil war, but the political struggle to dismantle his reforms continued. The resistance came from multiple factions, not simply the populares, though they were among the most vocal. Some wanted the powers of the tribunes restored, arguing that Sulla had silenced the voice of the people and handed too much authority to the Senate. Ambitious young nobles resented the fact that these reforms limited their advancement, and wealthy non-senators wanted influence in the courts returned to them.

In 73 BCE, Caesar was appointed to the College of Pontiffs, becoming a pontifex. This was a prestigious office, increasing his public standing and influence considerably. Around the same time, he was elected military tribune, a common early step for young aristocrats. Military tribunes served as staff officers and junior commanders rather than independent field commanders. It was a useful position for building connections and creating visibility.

The Third Servile War broke out in 73 BCE when enslaved people led by Spartacus rebelled and ravaged much of southern Italy. The revolt was ultimately crushed by Marcus Licinius Crassus, with the famous general Pompey playing a supporting role in its final stages. Caesar did not play any meaningful part in suppressing the rebellion, but he did begin to develop a relationship with Crassus during this period. Crassus would later prove important to his career.

Caesar used his connection to Marius publicly and aligned himself with those pushing to reverse Sulla's reforms. He also became a vocal supporter of Pompey, who was, at that point, the most prominent Roman general. However, Pompey had a history of fighting against the Marian cause. Pompey had helped defeat Sertorius in Spain, who had established an independent state loyal to the Marian faction, and had suppressed the revolt of Lepidus in 77 BCE when the consul attempted to overturn Sulla's settlement by force. Nevertheless, Caesar recognized that Pompey's military prestige made him a powerful political force.

In 70 BCE, Pompey and Crassus were elected consuls. Both opposed key elements of Sulla's constitution. During their consulship, the powers of the tribunate were largely restored. Caesar's influence was rising steadily during this period, building his support base through charm, ambition, and strategic alliances. He was not yet a major political player, but he was becoming a recognizable figure in Roman public life.

The First Triumvirate. Left to right is Pompey, Crassus, and Caesar'

Masterful Politician

Caesar's connections, oratory, and political maneuvering allowed him to gain higher offices. In 69 BCE, he was elected quaestor. The office required him to serve under the proprietor (governor) of Hispania Ulterior in southern Spain. However, his time there was cut short by two deaths. His aunt Julia, the widow of Marius, died, as did his wife Cornelia, who had recently given birth to his only daughter, Julia. Caesar returned to Rome to deliver both eulogies. At his aunt's funeral, he displayed images of Marius in public, something that had not been done since Sulla's victory in the civil war. It made him popular with ordinary Romans but caused considerable anger among senators who had suffered under Marius.

Ancient sources also record an anecdote from Caesar's time in Spain. While in what is now Cádiz, Caesar reportedly saw a statue of Alexander the Great and wept, struck by how much the Macedonian had accomplished at a young age. The story is reported by Plutarch but cannot be verified, so it may be a later invention.

Caesar's election as quaestor made him eligible to sit in the Senate. After Cornelia's death, he eventually married Pompeia, doing so around 67 BCE. Pompeia was connected to the family of Sulla, and the match may have been seen as a gesture of reconciliation between Caesar and the conservative Cornelii clan. The marriage produced no children, and Caesar started to become notorious during this period for his extramarital affairs.

In 65 BCE, he was elected curule aedile. The office gave him responsibility for the day-to-day administration of Rome and allowed him to act as a patron to a large number of clients. Patronage was central to Roman political life, and many of the ties Caesar cultivated during this period remained loyal to him throughout his career. He organized lavish games, such as gladiatorial combat, animal hunts, and other popular entertainment, which made him enormously popular with the Roman public. As you could probably guess, a political career was expensive, and Caesar fell heavily into debt financing his ambitions. He also restored the trophies and images of Marius, a move that his enemies attacked in the Senate.

Around the same time, the Senate passed the Lex Gabinia in 67 BCE, granting Pompey sweeping powers to deal with the pirate threat. Pirates, operating mainly from Cilicia, had disrupted Rome's grain supply and coastal trade to a serious degree. This law gave Pompey authority over any area within fifty miles of the sea, the ability to raise funds, and the power to appoint legates without consultation. It was an extraordinary grant of power. Pompey moved quickly and crushed the pirates in a matter of months. Then, in 66 BCE, the Lex Manilia granted him command of the Roman legions in the East, replacing Lucius Licinius Lucullus, whose exhausted troops had become increasingly resistant to further campaigning. Caesar supported both measures, though many did so. Pompey went on to defeat Mithridates and extend Roman power as far as Judea. It was during this period that he became known as Pompey the Great.

In 63 BCE, Caesar sought election as Pontifex Maximus, the chief priest of Rome. He would be responsible for overseeing the city's religious observances and traditions. It was a highly prestigious office. Among his rivals was the conservative senator Catulus. Caesar's candidacy was met with some skepticism. Despite his priestly office, he was not known for his piety, and his outlook on religion was more rationalistic, which was common among educated Romans of his class. He won regardless. His enemies claimed he had bribed the electors, which was entirely possible. Although Caesar had fallen deeply into debt by this point, bribery and vote-buying were a standard feature of Roman political life. He was far from alone in practicing this. The title Pontifex Maximus was later passed to Roman emperors and was eventually adopted by the bishop of Rome.

That same year, he was elected praetor for 62 BCE, one of the Roman Republic's senior offices. This double victory showed that, despite growing suspicion among conservatives, he had built a real following in Rome.

A bust of Cicero.[5]

Political Scandal and Conspiracy

If Caesar was expecting an easy time, he was wrong. The year 62 BCE proved to be a turbulent year for him. As Pontifex Maximus, he and his household resided in the official residence on the Via Sacra. His wife Pompeia had religious duties that included hosting the Festival of the

Bona Dea, a ceremony restricted to women. The notorious Publius Clodius allegedly disguised himself as a woman and entered the house during the festival. The scandal was huge. Clodius was arrested and charged with impiety. Caesar declined to testify against him and did not pursue a prosecution. He did, however, divorce Pompeia. When asked why, he reportedly said that his wife must be above suspicion—a phrase that has passed into common usage. By divorcing Pompeia, he distanced himself from the scandal and signaled that any impropriety was unacceptable in his household.

The same year saw the Catilinarian conspiracy. Lucius Sergius Catilina (better known in English as simply Catiline), having failed to win the consulship, gathered a force of supporters and attempted to overthrow the elected government. The conspiracy was uncovered by the consul Cicero, who moved swiftly against it. The ringleaders in Rome, including Lentulus and Cethegus, were arrested. Catiline himself fled and was killed in battle in 62 BCE.

In the Senate, Caesar spoke in favor of caution. He argued against the summary execution of the conspirators held in Rome on the grounds that it would be controversial. The Senate's emergency decree, the *senatus consultum ultimum*, gave broad powers, but it did not explicitly extend to executing Roman citizens without trial, making this a matter of genuine legal dispute. Caesar proposed instead that the conspirators be detained in Italian towns and their property confiscated. It was an unusual proposal. Rome did not typically use long-term detention as a punishment, and the logistics would be difficult. Cato the Younger argued forcefully for execution and prevailed. The conspirators were put to death.

Caesar's enemies claimed he had been involved in the conspiracy itself. This was almost certainly political slander. Some modern scholars have questioned aspects of Cicero's account and whether the threat was as grave as he presented it, but most believe that the conspiracy was real. Caesar's opposition to the executions was more likely rooted in legal principle and political calculation than in sympathy for them. His stance earned him some new supporters and presented him as a voice for moderation at a time when Romans had grown weary of political violence. Whether it won him more than it cost him is difficult to say. He was still a controversial figure by the end of 62 BCE. He had built a broad support base, but many conservatives deeply distrusted him.

Battles in Spain

After his praetorship, Caesar was appointed governor of Hispania Ulterior, where he had previously served as quaestor. He governed with proconsular imperium, though his formal rank was propraetor. Proconsular imperium is the legal authority given to Roman officers to govern provinces outside of Rome. He commanded the provincial forces available to him and raised additional troops as needed. It was his first independent military command. He had watched how Pompey and Marius had built their careers on military reputation, and he needed victories and money. A provincial command offered both.

Roman control over the Iberian Peninsula was well established in most areas, though the northwest remained less firmly under Roman authority. Caesar moved against the tribes of that region. Among them were the Gallaeci, who inhabited what is now Galicia in the northwest. He invaded their territory using a combination of land forces and a fleet to maintain supply lines, moving quickly through difficult terrain. He subdued the Gallaeci and pushed on to the Atlantic coast. He also campaigned against the Lusitanians in what is now Portugal, subduing them as well. These victories led his troops to hail him as imperator, a title given to a successful general and a necessary step toward claiming a triumph in Rome. He exaggerated the significance of his victories somewhat—the northwest was not fully pacified—but they still enhanced his standing in Rome.

His victories also qualified him for a triumph. This presented a problem. To celebrate a triumph, a general had to remain outside the city boundary, the *pomerium*, until the ceremony. But to declare his candidacy for the consulship, he had to appear in person in Rome. He could not do both. His conservative opponents, led by Cato the Younger, refused any accommodation and insisted that Caesar abide by tradition. Caesar chose the consulship and abandoned the triumph. It was a pragmatic decision, though it added to his grievances against Cato and the conservative faction.

Rise to Power

Caesar declared his candidacy for the consulship of 59 BCE. The field included several candidates. Caesar campaigned effectively. His oratory was persuasive, and he had support across different factions, in part because he had presented himself as a moderate rather than a partisan. He needed money, though, so he turned to Crassus. He also sought to coordinate with Lucius Lucceius, a wealthy aristocrat who was also running for consul, in hopes of pooling resources. Ultimately, Caesar won. The second consulship went to Bibulus, a staunch conservative and political opponent of Caesar, which complicated matters from the start.

Before taking office, Caesar had already set about building the political foundation he would need. Crassus and Pompey distrusted each other and had clashed before. So, Caesar brokered an informal arrangement between them. Modern historians call this the First Triumvirate, though it was not officially recognized by the Senate. It was a private practical alliance. Pompey brought military prestige and veteran soldiers who needed land. Crassus brought money. Caesar brought political skill, popular support, and his connections with the populares. He was the least powerful of the three in military terms, but he was the one who made the alliance function. Also, as Pontifex Maximus, Caesar held Rome's highest religious office. While magistrates were the ones who formally consulted omens before public meetings, his position still gave him influence over religious matters that could affect politics.

Caesar had come a long way. Until this point, his career had been more political than military. That was about to change.

Chapter 3: First Consulship and the Gallic Wars

Caesar's Political Genius

Caesar used his consulship to push through significant reforms. The Roman constitution required laws to be passed by the popular assemblies rather than the Senate, though Senate support was essential to pass anything. The alliance with Crassus and Pompey gave him the muscle to overcome the factional deadlock that had blocked reform for years.

He had the Senate's proceedings published for the first time, making its business visible to ordinary Romans. Pompey needed land for his veterans, and Caesar delivered it with a land distribution bill. Crassus wanted relief for his tax-farming clients in the provinces, and Caesar adjusted the taxation system. In return, both men backed his consulship.

Conservatives in the Senate, led by Cato the Younger, bitterly opposed all of it. Caesar's fellow consul, Bibulus, attempted to block the legislation through obstruction and by invoking religious technicalities, declaring that the omens were unfavorable and that no public business could lawfully proceed. Caesar ignored these declarations and pressed ahead, bringing his land bill before the popular assembly. Tensions quickly escalated. When Bibulus tried to intervene in person, violence broke out among the crowd. His attendants were attacked, and Bibulus was forced to flee. Humiliated and unable to stop Caesar, Bibulus withdrew to his house, where he spent the remainder of the year issuing formal protests that were largely ignored.

The First Triumvirate dominated Roman politics that year, though significant opposition remained. Caesar cemented his relationship with Pompey further by giving him his daughter Julia in marriage. It seemed the two men had a genuinely close bond.

During his consulship, Caesar also passed the Lex Julia de Repetundis, a law cracking down on corruption in the provinces. Governors had long been accused of exploiting the people under their rule, enriching themselves at Rome's expense. Caesar's law tightened the rules and made it easier to prosecute those who abused their power. It was one of his more lasting achievements, surviving long after many of his other controversial measures had faded.

When his consulship ended, Caesar moved quickly to secure his position. He and his supporters passed a law granting him an extraordinary provincial command. He would have proconsular authority over Illyricum, Cisalpine Gaul, and Transalpine Gaul with a term of five years. Multi-year commands were not entirely without precedent—Pompey had received similar arrangements—but the combination of three provinces and multiple legions was unusual. Caesar left for these provinces as soon as his consulship expired. As a private citizen in Rome, he would have been vulnerable to prosecution by his enemies, and Cato the Younger had made it clear that he intended to pursue exactly that. Leaving was the safer option.

Also in 59 BCE, Caesar married Calpurnia, his third wife. She came from the powerful Piso family. Like his previous marriages, it was a political arrangement. It strengthened his ties with an important family at an important moment.

Map of Gaul during Caesar's invasion[6]

The War with the Germans

Caesar already held command of his provinces before any Gallic crisis emerged. When the opportunity for war presented itself the following year, he took it. Under Roman tradition, war had to be just. It had to be fought in defense of Rome or its allies. Caesar found his justification in the movements of the Helvetii, a Celtic people from what is now Switzerland, who migrated westward into Gaul in 58 BCE, allegedly under pressure from Germanic tribes to the east. Their migration threatened the Aedui, a tribe allied with Rome. Caesar intervened, framing the campaign as a defense of Roman allies rather than outright conquest.

He expanded his forces before moving against the Helvetii, raising additional legions. He intercepted them near Bibracte and positioned his legions on high ground with the baggage train behind them. The Helvetii attacked directly. The legions' throwing javelins broke up the assault, and even the arrival of allied reinforcements, including the Boii, could not turn the tide. The Helvetii were defeated and forced to return to their homeland. They retained a degree of autonomy but were now effectively subordinate to Rome.

Caesar then turned north. The Suebi, a Germanic people under their leader Ariovistus, had invaded the territory of the Aedui and the Sequani, pushing deep into Gaul. Ariovistus had previously been recognized by the Senate as a friend of Rome, but his continued expansion threatened Roman interests. Caesar marched his legions into Sequani territory. Negotiations were attempted, but they quickly broke down.

Ariovistus proved to be a capable strategist. He maneuvered his army behind the Roman forces, threatening their supply lines. For several days, neither side would commit to open battle. Eventually, his warriors, eager to fight, forced his hand. The Germans attacked. Their initial charge pushed the Roman lines hard. Caesar ordered the cavalry under Publius Crassus, the son of his ally, to strike at the exposed German flank. That charge broke their formation, and Roman infantry discipline did the rest. The Suebi were driven back across the Rhine.

Caesar reported that 120,000 of the enemy were killed. Modern historians treat such figures with considerable skepticism. Ancient commanders routinely inflated enemy losses, and Caesar would have been no exception. What is not in doubt is that in a single year, he had defeated two large forces and significantly extended Roman influence in Gaul.

Caesar was also a skilled propagandist. He sent regular dispatches back to Rome, where they were circulated and read publicly. These accounts were later compiled into the *Commentarii de Bello Gallico* (*Commentaries of the Gallic War*). They are considered a masterpiece of Latin prose. They are also, without question, a work of political self-promotion. Caesar's victories are presented in the best possible light, with his setbacks minimized or omitted entirely.

The Conquest of Gaul

Caesar returned to Transalpine Gaul, where he rested his troops, raised new recruits, and attended to the administration of his provinces. He also enlisted Gallic and German auxiliaries to supplement his cavalry. After the victories of 58 BCE, much of Gaul appeared open to conquest. And once again, local disputes gave him a reason to intervene.

The Belgae, a large tribal confederation inhabiting what is now Belgium and the surrounding region, began raiding a Roman ally. What made this threat unusual was its scale. The Belgic tribes had formed a rare inter-tribal coalition, and Caesar reported their combined numbers as enormous. These figures were almost certainly exaggerated, but they allowed him to present the campaign as defending Roman security rather than outright aggression. Caesar moved quickly. He marched to the main settlement of the Remi, a tribe that had allied itself with Rome, with a force of up to twenty thousand legionaries and an unknown number of allied troops.

The two sides faced each other across the River Aisne in a tense standoff. Caesar fortified his position and refused to be drawn into unfavorable ground. The Belgic coalition was vast and began to fracture. Shortages and internal divisions forced them to dissolve before a decisive engagement could take place.

Caesar pressed forward into Belgic territory anyway, despite dangerously overstretched supply lines. He laid siege to one of the tribe's major hillforts. The defenders, unfamiliar with Roman siege equipment, surrendered. Caesar then prudently withdrew to Roman-held territory.

On the return march, the legions were ambushed by the Nervii, one of the most formidable of the Belgic tribes, along with their allies. The Nervii struck while the Romans were still making camp, driving back the cavalry and light troops before the legions could form properly. The fighting was desperate, and Roman centurions fell in significant numbers. The lines came close to breaking entirely. Caesar took a shield and fought in the front ranks himself, a move that steadied his men. Fighting alongside their commander let them know that the battle could be won. Other Roman units that had advanced too far returned to the field in time to help. It was one of the most dangerous moments of Caesar's entire Gallic command. The Nervii were eventually defeated, but the battle showed how formidable Rome's enemies in the north could be.

The defeat of the Nervii broke the wider Belgic resistance. Most tribes submitted under harsh terms. The Aduatuci, who refused, were dealt with ruthlessly. Caesar claims tens of thousands were sold into slavery. The sale of captives generated enormous wealth for Caesar and his officers. Some Germanic tribes along the Rhine sought diplomatic contact with Rome, though the frontier remained unstable.

The year 57 BCE had been another year of significant victories. Caesar wintered his army in northern Gaul. The following year brought fresh trouble. Roman taxation and demands had pushed many Gallic tribes toward rebellion. The leaders of the revolt were the Veneti, a maritime people of what is now Brittany. They had detained Roman envoys, and they controlled the Atlantic trade routes of western Gaul. Their coastal hillforts made them almost impossible to subdue by land alone. If they were besieged in one, they could simply escape by sea to another.

Caesar needed a fleet. He forced his allies to help him build one capable of operating in Atlantic waters. The two fleets met in Quiberon Bay. The Roman ships were oar-powered, while the Veneti relied on sail. Caesar's sailors used hooks on long poles to catch and cut the Veneti rigging, disabling their ships and leaving them vulnerable to boarding. The Veneti, caught without wind and unable to maneuver, were overwhelmed. This is a great example of Roman adaptability, as Caesar had never commanded a fleet before. The defeat of the Veneti extended Rome's reach to the Atlantic coast and intimidated the remaining coastal tribes. Their leadership was executed, and the survivors were sold into slavery. Caesar's subordinates, including Publius Crassus, continued operations in the southwest and Normandy.

Much of Gaul had now submitted, at least formally. Caesar's army was becoming something more than a provincial force. It was battle-hardened, experienced in a dozen different kinds of terrain and enemy, and increasingly loyal to its commander rather than to Rome. That bond would matter greatly in the years ahead.

In 56 BCE, Caesar met with Crassus and Pompey at Lucca to renew their alliance. The meeting drew around two hundred senators. The three men agreed to support each other's ambitions. Pompey and Crassus would stand for the consulship again. Crassus would receive Syria, where the prospect of a war against the Parthians, a powerful Iranian empire, loomed. Pompey would receive Spain. Caesar's own command in Gaul was extended for another five years. This was no minor thing. It guaranteed continued imperium, which protected him from prosecution, and gave him the time and resources to complete the conquest.

However, tensions within the alliance were already growing. Conservative senators, Cato among them, were working to draw Pompey away from Caesar. Pompey still commanded enormous prestige in Rome. But Caesar's victories, and the wealth and loyalty they had generated, had made him a force that could no longer be ignored.

Crossing the Rhine and the First Invasion of England

In 55 BCE, Germanic tribes crossed the Rhine into Gaul, threatening the stability Caesar had spent years establishing. Rather than simply repel them, he decided to make a statement. He ordered his engineers to build a bridge across the Rhine. His men would not use boats; this would be a proper timber bridge driven into the riverbed. It was completed in ten days, stretching across one of the greatest rivers of the known world. Caesar crossed with his army and spent eighteen days raiding Germanic territory. He and his men burned the villages of tribes that refused to submit and then withdrew, demolishing the bridge behind them. Caesar had never intended to stay. The point was the crossing itself. He wanted to show the Germanic tribes that the Rhine was not a barrier to Roman power and that no one was beyond his reach.

That same year, Caesar made his first crossing to Britain. He took two legions, although they achieved little beyond a landing on the coast. They were forced back by storms and determined British resistance. It was, by his own standards, an unsatisfying result. Caesar returned the following year, 54 BCE, with a much larger force—five legions and two thousand cavalry carried in eight hundred ships. It was the largest amphibious operation in the history of the world at that point.

This time, the landing was unopposed. The Britons united under a capable warlord named Cassivellaunus, who realized he could not defeat Caesar in open battle and instead used chariot warfare and guerrilla tactics to slow the Roman advance. Caesar forced a crossing of the Thames, pushing into Cassivellaunus's territory north of the river. Rival British tribes, hostile to Cassivellaunus, provided intelligence that led Caesar to his stronghold.

Faced with the fall of his base and pressure from multiple directions, Cassivellaunus sued for peace. He handed over hostages and agreed to pay an annual tribute. Caesar left without leaving a single soldier behind. Whether the tribute was ever paid is unknown. Britain was not conquered, but Caesar had been there and forced its leading warlord to submit. In Rome, that was enough.

Caesar returned to Gaul to find the situation deteriorating, as even Roman allies hated the burden of occupation. The legions had to be fed by the local population, who could barely feed themselves. A poor harvest had made the situation even more desperate. Caesar was forced to scatter his legions across a wide area to avoid overburdening any single tribe. This left them isolated and vulnerable.

In the winter of 54 BCE, an Eburones chieftain named Ambiorix saw his opportunity. He approached the Roman commanders Sabinus and Cotta, who were wintering in Eburones territory with a legion and five cohorts (a unit of a legion that numbered around 480 men), and deceived them with a false warning. He told them all of Gaul was rising and that Germanic tribes were crossing the Rhine. He offered safe passage if they abandoned their camp. Sabinus, against the advice of his co-commander Cotta, accepted.

It was a catastrophic mistake. As the Roman column moved out, Ambiorix's men ambushed them in a ravine. The legion was virtually destroyed. Sabinus was killed attempting to negotiate, and Cotta fell fighting. A handful of survivors made their way to other Roman camps to report the disaster.

Ambiorix then moved against Quintus Cicero, the younger brother of the famous orator, who was wintering nearby with another legion. Unlike Sabinus, Cicero refused to be deceived and held his camp under a sustained siege that lasted weeks. His men suffered enormous casualties; by the end, nine out of ten had been wounded. Caesar moved to relieve him with whatever forces he could gather, marching his men hard through Nervii territory. He arrived in time. The Gauls abandoned the siege and were driven off.

It had been the most dangerous winter of the entire Gallic campaign and served as a reminder that the conquest of Gaul was far from complete.

A modern reimagining of Caesar's bridge over the Rhine.[7]

The Revolt of Rome and Vercingetorix

In 52 BCE, a young Arvernian nobleman named Vercingetorix achieved something remarkable. He persuaded the disunited tribes of Gaul to set aside their rivalries and unite against Rome. The various tribes swore to defend their lands and drive out the invaders. It was the most serious challenge to Roman rule since Caesar had first crossed into Gaul.

Caesar was in Cisalpine Gaul when the revolt broke out. He moved with his usual quick speed, crossing into Transalpine Gaul and launching an offensive through the south before the rebel alliance could fully organize. Vercingetorix knew he could not match the Romans in open battle. His strategy was to avoid direct confrontation, destroy food supplies, and starve the legions. His allies pushed him to fight, though, and at Avaricum—one of the most prosperous towns in Gaul and one of the few his allies had refused to burn as part of their scorched-earth strategy—Caesar laid siege and eventually stormed the walls. According to his own account, most of the population was massacred. It was a brutal demonstration of what resistance cost and a warning to the rest of Gaul.

Vercingetorix withdrew to Gergovia, the hilltop stronghold of the Arverni in what is now south-central France. It was a formidable position. Caesar moved against it and began building fortifications to cut it off, though the terrain made a complete encirclement impossible. When the Aedui tribe revolted and disrupted his supply lines, Caesar's position became precarious. Rather than lift the siege, he ordered an assault. It went badly. The attack broke down in confusion, and there was poor coordination between units. The Gallic defenders inflicted heavy casualties. Caesar later claimed he had not suffered a defeat, but his losses were severe enough that he was forced to withdraw. It was the lowest point of the entire campaign.

Vercingetorix gathered his forces at Alesia, a heavily fortified settlement on a plateau in what is now Burgundy. Caesar chose not to assault it directly. Instead, he ordered the construction of an enormous ring of fortifications around the town. In the end, there were over twenty miles of trenches, walls, towers, and an elaborate system of concealed pits and sharpened stakes designed to break any sortie from the garrison. At the same time, a vast Gallic relief army assembled and marched to break the siege. Caesar's response was to build a second ring of fortifications facing outward, protecting his army from an attack in the rear. His force now sat between the garrison inside Alesia and the relief army outside. Caesar's men were under attack from both directions, and the fighting was ferocious and continuous. Whether Vercingetorix had planned from the outset to draw Caesar into this position or had simply retreated to Alesia after his earlier reverses is debated by historians.

In the end, Roman discipline and engineering proved decisive. The Gallic relief army could not break through Caesar's outer fortifications. Supplies ran out inside Alesia. In desperation, Vercingetorix sent the women and children of the town out through the gates, hoping Caesar would let them pass or be moved to negotiate. Caesar refused. Trapped in the no-man's land between the two lines, many of them died of starvation and exposure. The relief army, unable to feed itself in the field, eventually scattered. With no hope of rescue, Vercingetorix surrendered. He rode out to Caesar and laid down his arms. He was taken to Rome, where he was held prisoner for years. He was eventually executed after Caesar's triumph.

The fall of Alesia broke Gallic resistance. The remaining tribes submitted, becoming clients of Rome or coming under direct Roman administration. Caesar had conquered a vast area of western Europe in less than a decade. However, the human cost was enormous. Ancient sources claim that millions died or were enslaved during the Gallic Wars, and some modern historians have described the campaign as genocidal in scale. The precise figures are impossible to verify because ancient casualty numbers are almost always exaggerated, but few serious scholars doubt that the wars caused a devastating loss of life across the region.

Vercingetorix surrendering to Caesar.[8]

Trouble Back Home

By 53 BCE, the First Triumvirate was close to collapse. Julia, Caesar's daughter and Pompey's wife, had died in childbirth. The personal bond between the two men pretty much died with her. Each grew suspicious of the other, and the alliance that had dominated Roman politics for years began to unravel.

Crassus, meanwhile, was increasingly aware that his partners had eclipsed him in military glory. He decided to fix this with a conquest of his own. Parthia, a powerful empire on Rome's eastern frontier, was his target. Crassus had military experience; he had served under Sulla in the civil wars of the 80s BCE and had crushed Spartacus decisively. However, he lacked the strategic brilliance and adaptability of men like Pompey and Caesar.

He led a force of roughly thirty-five thousand to forty thousand men into the East. The Parthians refused to meet him in a conventional engagement. Instead, a Parthian general named Surena drew the Romans into the open desert of what is now eastern Syria, near the town of Carrhae. There, he unleashed his cavalry. The mounted archers, for which Parthia was famous, were capable of shooting at full gallop and even backward at pursuing enemies. Surena kept his archers supplied by camel train, ensuring the volleys never stopped.

The Roman formation held for a time but had no answer for the harassment. When the Romans finally broke during the retreat, the Parthians pursued and destroyed much of the army. Around twenty thousand Romans were killed, and ten thousand were taken prisoner. Several thousand escaped to Syria. The Roman legionary standards were captured; this was a profound humiliation that Rome would not avenge for decades. They were not recovered until the reign of Augustus, who obtained them through diplomacy rather than force. Crassus himself was killed during a failed negotiation. Ancient sources, including Plutarch and Cassius Dio, claim that molten gold was poured into his mouth after his death, a commentary on his greed. Whether this is true is impossible to say, although it reads more like legend than history.

The Battle of Carrhae was more than a military disaster. It removed the man who had held the First Triumvirate together. Crassus had been the third pillar of the alliance. He was wealthy enough to fund both his partners and useful as a mediator between two men whose ambitions were pulling in opposite directions. Without him, the arrangement became a contest between Caesar and Pompey.

The Senate conservatives, led by Cato and others, recognized the opportunity. They began working on Pompey, flattering him, appealing to his pride, and positioning him as the defender of the Roman Republic against Caesar's growing power. Pompey, whose relationship with the conservative bloc had always been complicated, began to move in their direction.

The process accelerated in 52 BCE. The murder of the populist agitator Clodius on the Appian Way sparked serious street violence in Rome. Clodius was no ordinary politician. A fiery populist and former tribune, he had built a powerful following among the urban poor and commanded loyal street gangs who clashed regularly with his rivals. For years, Rome's politics had spilled out of the Senate and into the streets, where intimidation and violence were becoming common tools of power. Clodius had actually helped create this atmosphere.

When he was killed in a confrontation with the followers of his rival Milo, news of his death spread quickly. His supporters carried his body into the Forum, where anger turned to fury. The crowd used benches and furniture to build a funeral pyre inside the Senate House itself, burning it to the ground.

With elections already delayed and no consuls in office, the Senate found itself unable to restore control through normal means. In desperation, it took the extraordinary step of appointing Pompey as sole consul. This was a rare and controversial move that gave Pompey sweeping authority to stabilize the city.

It is important to note that this was legally sanctioned. It was not a dictatorship, but it marked a decisive shift. Pompey was now governing Rome with the backing of the conservative Senate. His break with Caesar was no longer a gradual drift; it was becoming a political reality. Rome was dividing into two camps: Pompey, who was aligned with the Senate, and Caesar, who commanded a loyal and battle-hardened army in Gaul. Both men were very powerful. Neither trusted the other. A confrontation was becoming very difficult to avoid.

Chapter 4: Crossing the Rubicon

In northern Italy flows the River Rubicon, a name derived from the Latin *rubico*, meaning "red," likely a reference to the reddish clay or mineral sediment that discolored its waters. On the morning of January 10th, 49 BCE, Julius Caesar crossed the Rubicon at the head of the Thirteenth Legion. His biographer Suetonius records that before crossing, Caesar declared, "Iacta alea est"—"The die is cast." It was the greatest gamble of his career.

The river's significance was legal as much as geographical. It marked the boundary between Cisalpine Gaul, which Caesar governed as his province, and the territory directly under the authority of the Senate. Roman law was clear on this point. A governor's imperium—his legal authority to command troops—applied only within his province. The moment he led armed forces across that line, his immunity evaporated. He became a private citizen under military command, which the Senate could treat as treason. This mattered enormously to Caesar. As long as he held imperium, he could not be prosecuted for his actions in Gaul. The moment he laid down his command and entered Rome as a private citizen, his enemies could (and likely would) put him on trial.

Cato and the conservative faction had spent years trying to maneuver Caesar into exactly that position. In early 49 BCE, the Senate demanded that Caesar disband his legions before his command formally expired. They then issued the *senatus consultum ultimum*, the emergency decree of last resort that effectively authorized the use of force against him. Caesar had no good options left. Crossing the river with his army was illegal. Submitting to the Senate meant ruin.

Caesar chose to cross. The phrase "crossing the Rubicon" is still used as a term for the point of no return.

The Senate moved quickly but had little to work with. Pompey's best troops were in Spain, and Italy itself was largely undefended. Rather than fight, the conservative faction fled Rome. This was not pure panic. Pompey wanted to regroup in the East, where he had deep networks of client states and loyal veterans. That way, he could defeat Caesar from a position of strength. It was a rational strategy, though it ceded Italy without a fight and badly damaged morale. Caesar's subordinates seized key positions across Italy while he marched south.

The road to the Rubicon stretched back several years. As mentioned, Julia, Caesar's daughter and Pompey's wife, had died in 54 BCE, which dissolved the personal bond between the two men. In 50 BCE, Caesar proposed that both he and Pompey disband their armies, which would have removed the military threat on both sides. The Senate, under the influence of the optimates, refused unless Caesar disarmed first. Pompey would not agree to mutual disarmament.

After his victory at Alesia, Caesar had petitioned the Senate to stand for the consulship in absentia; this means he would stand for consulship without giving up his command. The Senate refused. Cato the Younger and his allies also blocked him from celebrating a triumph.

Why Caesar chose to cross rather than negotiate or submit has been debated for centuries. Ancient sources, including Suetonius and Plutarch, tend to portray it as personal ambition. This was the act of a man who had always intended to make himself master of Rome. Modern historians are less certain. Some see Caesar acting defensively, protecting his dignitas and his political survival against enemies who left him no lawful way out. Others argue that he had long sought sole power and used the legal crisis as justification. Most likely, both were true to some

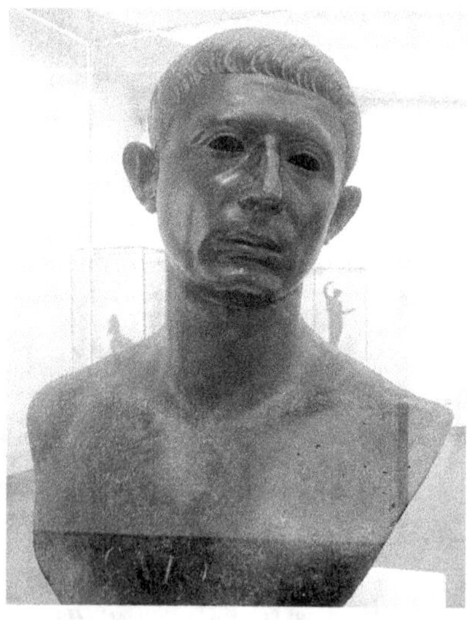

A bronze bust of Cato the Younger. '

degree. What is clear is that the Roman Republic's institutions had been under strain for decades.

Caesar's Civil War in Spain

Caesar now controlled Italy but faced Pompeian armies on multiple fronts, namely in Spain, Africa, and the Balkans. He also had to deal with Massalia, a powerful Greek city in what is now Marseille, which had declared neutrality but was effectively siding with Pompey. Caesar began the siege, left two capable generals in command to continue it, and turned his attention to Spain.

Before leaving Rome, Caesar attempted to access the state treasury to fund his campaign. A tribune named Metellus tried to block him. Caesar overrode this opposition and forced compliance. The episode was telling. Fighting a civil war was very expensive, and Caesar needed funds immediately. The treasury was the fastest source. That a tribune—theoretically a sacrosanct office, immune from force—could be brushed aside showed how far republican norms had already eroded. In Rome, Mark Antony was left in control of Italy, and Lepidus still served as praetor.

Spain was the main priority. Pompey had built his political base there over decades, and the legions in the peninsula were experienced veterans loyal to his cause. Control of Spain meant control of significant manpower and revenue—resources Caesar could not leave in enemy hands while he pursued Pompey in the East.

The Pompeian legates Lucius Afranius and Marcus Petreius held Hispania Citerior with veteran forces and had seized much of the northwest. Caesar marched quickly, raised additional troops, and moved against their position on the River Segre near Ilerda (known today as Lleida). The fighting was hard. Both sides were experienced, morale was strained, and there were even instances of soldiers from opposing sides communicating with each other. The decisive move came when Caesar ordered trenches to be dug to divert the river, threatening to cut the Pompeians off from their supply lines. Unnerved, the republican forces retreated, but Caesar surrounded them before they could reach safety. Facing no escape, the Pompeian legions surrendered. Most were disarmed and dismissed rather than incorporated into Caesar's ranks.

With Spain secured, Caesar could turn his full attention to Pompey in the East.

Siege of Massalia and the Campaign in North Africa

The siege of Massalia had continued in Caesar's absence under the command of Gaius Trebonius on land and Decimus Junius Brutus Albinus at sea. The defenders put up a determined resistance. At one point, during a negotiated truce, they set fire to the Roman siege works. This bought them time, but it did not change the outcome. The city surrendered in September 49 BCE. Caesar was not there, but he had already ordered that Massalia should not be sacked and that the inhabitants should be treated with restraint.

The situation in Africa was more damaging. The province was strategically vital for reasons that went beyond its geography. It supplied a significant portion of Rome's grain and controlled sea routes between Italy and the western Mediterranean. A hostile force based there could threaten Sicily and Italy directly. If Africa fell into Pompeian hands, it could be a base from which eastern and western forces could coordinate against Caesar. The war was already becoming an international struggle.

Caesar entrusted the African campaign to Gaius Scribonius Curio, an able politician but an inexperienced general. Curio landed with a huge force and moved against the Pompeian commander Publius Attius Varus, who held the city and port of Utica. Curio defeated Varus in battle near the city and then began a siege. The Caesarians also captured much of the enemy fleet.

However, Varus held on, knowing that help was on the way. Juba I, king of Numidia, was a firm ally of Pompey and had his own reasons to oppose Caesar. Curio had previously proposed a law to annex his kingdom outright. Juba's cavalry was widely considered among the finest in the region, and he was now marching to relieve Utica.

What followed exposed Curio's inexperience. He received conflicting reports about the size of Juba's force. It was first reported that it was enormous, but then he heard that only a small advance detachment was nearby. Curio abandoned the siege, withdrew to the coast, and then advanced inland to strike what he believed was a manageable enemy.

It was a trap. The full Numidian army was waiting. At the Battle of the Bagradas, fought in the August heat on open ground, Curio's legionaries were worn down by the conditions and outmaneuvered by Juba's cavalry. The Roman force was destroyed, and Curio died fighting rather than abandoning his men. Juba executed many of the Roman prisoners, including several senators. Only a few of Caesar's soldiers made it back to Sicily. It was the worst Caesarian defeat of the opening phase of the war, and it showed that Caesar's cause was heavily dependent on Caesar himself. His lieutenants, however capable they were in politics, were not always great in the field. The defeat strengthened Pompeian morale in Africa and secured the province as a Pompeian base for years to come.

Caesar the Dictator

Caesar returned to Rome in December 49 BCE. Marcus Aemilius Lepidus, as praetor, proposed a law appointing him dictator by constitutional procedure. The dictatorship was an ancient office. It was reserved for national emergencies, and it gave that person extraordinary authority within Rome and Italy.

He then stood for the consulship himself and was elected for 48 BCE. After eleven days, he resigned the dictatorship. He had regained his imperium legally and was now free to pursue Pompey.

Caesar spent his short dictatorship holding consular elections, restoring administrative continuity after the Senate's flight, and passing urgent legislation, including the restoration of political rights to the descendants of Sulla's proscription victims. Caesar used it for exactly that and then resigned from the office.

It is important to distinguish this brief, constitutionally grounded appointment from what came later. Caesar would be appointed dictator again in 48, 46, and 44 BCE, each time with broader powers and fewer constraints. The last appointment, in early 44 BCE, made him dictator perpetuo—dictator in perpetuity, meaning he had no time limit. It was that appointment, not the emergency measure of 49 BCE, that truly broke with republican tradition and triggered the conspiracy that killed him.

Even so, many Romans were alarmed from the start. The comparison to Sulla, who had used the same office to carry out mass proscriptions and restructure the constitution, was impossible to avoid. Plus, Caesar had spent years criticizing exactly that precedent. His response was a policy of clemency. He pardoned enemies, released prisoners, and made it clear that Sulla's bloodbath would not be repeated. He did not do this purely out of the kindness of his heart. Caesar understood that clemency—*clementia Caesaris,* as it came to be known—was sound politics. Proscriptions would have made him feared and hated. It would have driven moderates into his enemies' camp. Restraint made him appear as a restorer of order rather than a tyrant. Many senators who had fled with Pompey had done so not out of deep ideological conviction but out of fear of being caught on the wrong side. Caesar gave them a way to come back.

The political situation was stabilizing, but the military picture remained uncertain. The war was becoming increasingly expensive. Caesar had forced access to the Roman treasury before leaving for Spain, but revenues from the provinces and the spoils of Gaul could only go so far. Pompey, by contrast, had retreated to the eastern Mediterranean, where the wealthiest provinces of the Roman world lay. The East offered far greater financial resources, a stronger naval capacity, and access to the manpower of client kingdoms stretching from Greece to Syria. Pompey likely calculated that he could sustain a long war of attrition from this base, grinding Caesar down while building an army large enough to retake the west.

The Battle of Pharsalus

At this point, Caesar was at the height of his powers. He was also known for his extraordinary physical endurance. He fought in the front rank, shared the hardships of his men, and intervened personally at critical moments on the battlefield. Ancient sources suggest he suffered from some form of seizure disorder, though the nature of his condition is debated by historians. His soldiers were devoted to him, and that loyalty had been forged over years of hard campaigning.

By the summer of 48 BCE, Pompey commanded a large army in Macedonia. The senators who had fled Rome regarded themselves as the legitimate Roman government and had established a functioning political body in exile.

The anti-Caesarian position was strong. Caesar did not have enough ships to transport his full army, and it took weeks to land his forces on the Albanian coast. He then advanced on Dyrrachium (modern Durres), which was Pompey's main base in the region. It was supplied continuously from the eastern Mediterranean. Control of it meant control of Pompey's ability to sustain his army in the field. Caesar understood this. Rather than bypass it, he moved to cut it off.

What followed was one of the most unusual episodes of the war. Unable to take Dyrrachium by force, Caesar ordered his engineers to build an enormous line of fortifications encircling Pompey's position. This was one of the largest field fortification systems constructed in the ancient world. Pompey responded by building counter-walls. The two armies ended up facing each other across miles of engineered earthworks, with the smaller Caesarian force attempting to contain the larger Pompeian army. It was siege warfare in reverse.

The operations lasted months. Both sides launched raids and counter-attacks. The besieging legions suffered from supply shortages and disease. Eventually, Gallic deserters revealed an underdefended section of Caesar's lines to Pompey. The Pompeians launched a concentrated assault, broke through, and came close to routing the Caesarian force entirely. Mark Antony helped stabilize the situation, and Caesar appeared in person to steady his men. The line held, but the position was untenable. Caesar eventually withdrew, covering the retreat by leaving two legions behind to follow later.

Dyrrachium was the worst defeat of his career, but Pompey chose not to pursue. This is widely regarded as his greatest mistake of the war. Had he pressed the attack, Caesar's army might not have survived. Instead, Caesar withdrew intact into Thessaly and began looking for a chance to force a decisive engagement on his own terms.

Caesar fell back because he was short on supplies and had to forage from the local population. When the city of Gomphi refused to open its gates, he besieged and took it quickly, allowing his soldiers to plunder it as punishment. It was harsh and unusual for Caesar, but it served its purpose, as the surrounding communities submitted rather than face the same treatment.

The conservative senators with Pompey grew impatient. Pompey's strategy had always favored attrition. He had the larger force, the stronger supply lines, and the wealth of the eastern provinces behind him. Time, in theory, would work in his favor. But the senators who had followed him into exile wanted a decisive battle and to return to Rome. They pressed him relentlessly, and some questioned whether he was prolonging the war to preserve his own command. This created tension between military prudence and political legitimacy; the men who considered themselves the rightful government of Rome could not afford to look as though they were hiding from a wanted criminal. Under all of this pressure, Pompey advanced to battle Caesar.

The two armies met on the plains near Pharsalus in Thessaly in August 48 BCE. Caesar had roughly twenty-two thousand infantry. Pompey had around forty thousand to forty-five thousand, along with a massive cavalry. He had approximately seven thousand horsemen against Caesar's one thousand. The key question was whether Pompey's cavalry could sweep around Caesar's flank and collapse his line.

Caesar anticipated this, though. He quietly assembled a fourth line of seasoned infantry behind his right wing and kept them hidden. When Pompey's cavalry charged and drove Caesar's horsemen back, these infantrymen moved forward and attacked the cavalry at close quarters, targeting the riders' faces with their javelins. The tactic worked. The cavalry broke and fled, exposing Pompey's left flank. Caesar then committed his reserves, who crashed into the exposed position. Pompey's line buckled and collapsed. His men fled to the camp, but the camp fell too. Caesar's men pursued Pompey and his men until nightfall.

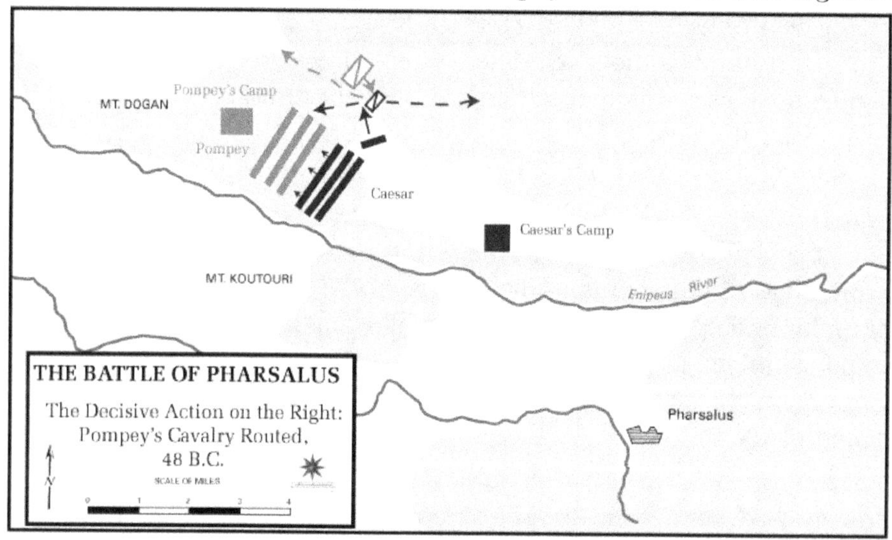

Map outlining actions of the Battle of Pharsalus. [10]

Pharsalus destroyed Pompey's field army, but it did not end the war. Still, it had fundamentally changed its character. Before Pharsalus, the conflict had been a genuine contest between two Roman commanders with comparable resources and legitimacy. After it, the Pompeian cause was reduced to scattered resistance. There were Cato and Metellus Scipio in Africa, holdouts in Spain, and Pompey himself fleeing eastward without an army. Caesar was no longer fighting a civil war between equals. He was hunting down the remnants of an opposition that had lost its military center of gravity.

In the aftermath, Caesar demonstrated his characteristic clemency toward Roman citizens who surrendered. He burned Pompey's correspondence without reading it rather than using it to identify and punish his enemies. Many senators surrendered and were pardoned, something that struck contemporaries as remarkable. The policy was politically calculated. It reduced further resistance and encouraged defections. It did not, however, end the war.

Chapter 5: Caesar and Cleopatra

War in Egypt

Pompey's destination was Egypt. It was a reasonable choice. Egypt was wealthy, its rulers owed him political debts, and it lay beyond Caesar's immediate reach. Pompey had connections there going back years. For instance, he was the one who helped restore Ptolemy XII to his throne after he had been driven out by his own people. Pompey expected gratitude. He miscalculated badly.

Egypt was ruled by the Ptolemies, a Macedonian dynasty founded by one of Alexander the Great's generals. By this point, it was effectively a client state of Rome. Ptolemy XII had borrowed enormous sums from Roman financiers to secure his restoration, leaving his successors with debts they could not repay. Now his young son, Ptolemy XIII, shared the throne (uneasily) with his sister and co-ruler Cleopatra VII. The two were at war with each other, and real power in the court sat with Ptolemy's regent, Pothinus, and the general Achillas, who, between them, dominated the young king entirely.

When Pompey's ship approached the Egyptian shore near Pelusium in September 48 BCE, he was invited to land. A small boat came out to meet him, carrying a former Roman officer now in Egyptian service. Pompey stepped in. He was stabbed to death before he reached the shore. Pothinus and his allies had decided that a Roman general on the losing side of a civil war was a liability, not an asset. Killing him was meant to demonstrate loyalty to Caesar and secure his favor.

It did not have that effect. Caesar arrived in Alexandria days later and was presented with Pompey's severed head and his signet ring. According to ancient accounts, he wept. Whether his grief was genuine is a question ancient sources raise but do not settle. Plutarch describes him as visibly shaken while leaving room for doubt about his sincerity. What is not in doubt is that Caesar understood the political problem. He had spent two years building a reputation for clemency. Being seen to profit from the murder of his greatest rival—a man who had once been his ally, his son-in-law's father, and one of Rome's most celebrated generals—would undermine everything he had worked to project. He arranged for Pompey's remains to receive proper burial rites and made it clear that the killers would face consequences.

Caesar remained in Alexandria. He had practical reasons for this. Egypt owed substantial debts to Rome stemming from the reign of Ptolemy XII, and Caesar needed money to keep his army in the field. He also announced he would decide the dispute between Ptolemy XIII and Cleopatra, citing a clause in their father's will. It was a Roman asserting Roman authority over a client kingdom, which was entirely in keeping with how Rome handled its dependencies. However, elements within the Alexandrian court resented it deeply.

Trapped in Alexander

Caesar moved into the royal palace and summoned both Ptolemy XIII and Cleopatra to present themselves before him. Ptolemy arrived, accompanied by Pothinus. Cleopatra could not. Her brother's forces controlled the city, and traveling openly to the palace would have meant almost certain death. So, she found another way. According to ancient sources, she had herself smuggled into the palace hidden inside a rolled carpet or linen sack, carried by a loyal servant past her brother's guards and into Caesar's presence.

Cleopatra was around twenty-one or twenty-two years old. Caesar was in his early fifties. She was, by all accounts, formidable. She was educated, politically astute, and fluent in multiple languages. She was notably the first ruler of her dynasty to learn Egyptian, setting her apart from all her Ptolemaic predecessors. The two became lovers.

When Ptolemy XIII discovered his sister was in the palace with Caesar, he flew into a rage and attempted to incite a riot among the Alexandrians. Caesar had him arrested. He then publicly announced that he would honor their father's will, declaring Ptolemy and Cleopatra joint rulers, which temporarily calmed the crowd.

It did not calm Pothinus. Caesar uncovered a plot between Pothinus and Achillas and had Pothinus executed. Achillas, who was already with the army outside the city, responded by marching on Alexandria. The siege had begun.

Caesar had arrived with around four thousand men, which was enough to project authority but not enough to fight a sustained urban siege. He sent urgent messages to his allies requesting relief. His survival depended on one thing: control of the harbor. He held part of the fleet and kept the sea lanes open through a combination of naval skirmishes and the tenacity of his soldiers. Without that lifeline, there was no prospect of reinforcement and no way out.

During the initial fighting around the harbor, Caesar ordered enemy ships burned to prevent their use against him. The fire spread to the waterfront. Ancient sources report that some books stored near the docks were destroyed in the blaze. Whether the great Library of Alexandria itself was damaged remains unclear, as the sources conflict with each other. What is known is that the fire at the harbor was a military decision, not a deliberate act of cultural destruction.

Bust of Cleopatra.[11]

The siege ground on. The Romans held their position but were hard-pressed by land and sea, barely keeping communications open across Alexandria's harbor. This was one of the most dangerous episodes of Caesar's career, and much of the danger was self-inflicted. He chose to entangle himself in Egypt's dynastic struggle with too few troops to control it.

Arsinoe, Cleopatra's younger sister, escaped from the palace and attached herself to the besieging army. The general Achillas was killed by her faction, and a eunuch named Ganymedes took command in his place. Arsinoe proved capable, and her presence gave the opposition renewed focus and unity. However, at some point during the siege, the Alexandrians must have grown frustrated with her leadership and petitioned Caesar to release Ptolemy XIII, offering Arsinoe in exchange.

Caesar agreed. He may have calculated that Ptolemy's presence in the rebel camp would fracture the opposition, that rival factions would turn on each other once the figurehead was among them. His officers argued against it, but Caesar overruled them. Ptolemy walked free and immediately rejoined the besieging forces. The attacks intensified. In the account later circulated under Caesar's name (it was almost certainly written by his officer Aulus Hirtius), the decision is defended, but the reasoning has not convinced many readers, ancient or modern.

The wider war was not standing still either. In Africa, the Pompeian forces under Cato and Metellus Scipio had regrouped and grown stronger in the wake of Pharsalus. In Spain, Pompeian commanders were regaining ground. In the Adriatic, a Pompeian fleet was operating freely and threatening supply lines to Italy. Caesar, the conqueror of Gaul, was pinned down in a palace in Alexandria by a conflict he had stumbled into through his own misjudgments.

Victory in Egypt

Relief came in early 47 BCE. Mithridates of Pergamum gathered a substantial force, crossed the Sinai into Egypt, and captured the key port of Pelusium. This was the breakthrough Caesar needed. Pelusium controlled the main land corridor from Syria into Egypt, and its fall forced Ptolemy XIII to divide his forces between containing Mithridates and maintaining the siege of Alexandria. Caesar was no longer isolated. He moved quickly to link up with his ally and took command of the combined force.

The decisive engagement came at the Battle of the Nile in February 47 BCE. A substantial Egyptian force, with some Pompeian elements, took up a defensive position in the Nile Delta region. Caesar was cautious about a frontal assault. The Egyptian heavy infantry was formidable, and they had a small naval force operating on the river. Control of the water determined who could move and who could not.

He chose an indirect approach instead. He sent engineers to find a suitable crossing point upstream, established a bridgehead away from the Egyptian lines, and built a pontoon bridge. His Gallic and German cavalry—veterans of the Gallic Wars now serving in his eastern force— crossed and attacked the Egyptian army from the rear. The infantry, armed with long spears, could not maneuver quickly enough to meet the threat. The Egyptian line collapsed. Ptolemy XIII fled and drowned in the Nile while attempting to escape. Caesar returned to Alexandria. The city submitted without a fight.

Caesar remained in Egypt for several months after the victory. He had practical reasons for staying. Cleopatra's position needed to be stabilized before he could safely leave. Installing a friendly ruler on Egypt's throne was one thing, but securing her against internal opposition was another. Egypt's grain supply and finances also required attention, and Caesar needed to ensure that the kingdom's resources would flow toward Rome rather than against it. He was also positioning himself diplomatically in the East, where client kingdoms needed to understand where Roman authority now sat.

A 17th-century etching of the Battle of the Nile. [18]

During this period, Caesar traveled the Nile with Cleopatra in a display of royal spectacle. Months later, she gave birth to a son she named Ptolemy Caesar, also known as Caesarion. Cleopatra presented the child as Caesar's heir. Caesar did not legally adopt the child or name him his heir. He neither publicly claimed nor repudiated the boy.

At this stage, the succession question was not yet the explosive issue it would later become. Caesar had not designated any heir, and the political crisis around Caesarion only fully ignited after Caesar's assassination, when Octavian's position as named heir in Caesar's will made Caesarion a potential rival. Under Augustus, the existence of a living son of Caesar and Cleopatra became genuinely dangerous, and Caesarion was eventually killed on Augustus's orders. Roman aristocratic culture was deeply suspicious of Eastern monarchy, and a child born outside Roman law to an Egyptian queen had no realistic path to formal recognition as a Roman heir anyway. However, some in Rome feared the implications of the child's existence. Others denied he was Caesar's son at all.

Caesar left Egypt in the summer of 47 BCE. He had been absent from the wider war for months, and the situation had deteriorated. Mark Antony, managing affairs in Rome as Caesar's deputy, was struggling to maintain order. Italy was restive, and the Pompeian forces in Africa under Cato and Metellus Scipio had only continued to strengthen.

In 46 BCE, Cleopatra traveled to Rome with Caesarion and stayed as Caesar's guest. It was a very unpopular move. Roman aristocratic opinion was hostile to foreign monarchs at the best of times, and Cleopatra's presence and her relationship with the most powerful man in Rome alarmed many. Her position had been considerably strengthened by Caesar's support. Egypt remained within Rome's sphere of influence, but Cleopatra was no longer simply a dependent client. She had leverage, and she used it skillfully to expand Egyptian influence in the Levant. The political implications of her relationship with Caesar were not lost on anyone in Rome.

I Came, I Saw, I Conquered

One of Rome's most formidable enemies had been Mithridates VI of Pontus, who fought three wars against Rome and at one point drove Roman forces out of Asia Minor entirely. In 88 BCE, he ordered the massacre of tens of thousands of Roman and Italian citizens across Asia Minor in a single coordinated attack. This event is known as the Asiatic Vespers, and it made him the most hated enemy in the East that Rome had ever faced. He was eventually brought down not by Rome but by his own son, Pharnaces II, who led a revolt against him. Mithridates VI attempted suicide when the revolt succeeded. However, the poison failed. He was killed by a bodyguard on his own orders.

In 63 BCE, Pharnaces II became ruler of the Bosporan Kingdom, centered in what is now Crimea, which was nominally a client of Rome. The civil war gave him his opportunity. Caesar's veteran legions were committed in Egypt or preparing for the African campaign. The forces available to Rome in Asia Minor were limited, and Pharnaces knew it. With Caesar trapped in Alexandria and no credible Roman army nearby to oppose him, Pharnaces II recruited a large force and moved into Armenia and Cappadocia, seizing territory including cities under direct Roman control. Ancient sources accuse him of harsh reprisals against the populations he conquered, including the mutilation of prisoners.

Caesar, who was still in Egypt, ordered Gnaeus Domitius Calvinus to take command of Roman forces in Asia Minor and deal with the threat. Calvinus gathered what troops he could, supplemented by forces from local rulers who had their own reasons to oppose Pharnaces.

It was not enough. The Romans were defeated at the Battle of Nicopolis in 48 BCE. Calvinus managed to get his legion off the field, but Pharnaces was now free to range through northern Asia Minor largely unchecked. His advance was only halted when his deputy in Crimea revolted, forcing him to return east and suppress the rebellion.

Pharnaces dealt with the revolt quickly and returned to Armenia in 47 BCE, confident he could consolidate his gains before Caesar could respond. He miscalculated. Caesar marched with extraordinary speed from Egypt through Syria and into Asia Minor, assembling legions and allied detachments as he went. Pharnaces attempted to buy time. He offered bribes and even proposed a marriage alliance. Caesar negotiated while preparing for battle. He advanced to high ground near Zela in what is now northern Turkey. His men began constructing their usual fortified camp on the elevated position.

Before they could finish, Pharnaces ordered his army to attack uphill. It was a bold and unconventional decision. Some historians believe he wanted to catch the Romans while they were still unprepared and in disorder. Pharnaces deployed scythed chariots at the front of the assault. The chariots initially caused disruption, but the disciplined Roman infantry used their javelins to bring down the drivers and neutralize the threat. The attack stalled.

Caesar's legionaries then pushed downhill into the Bosporan force and routed it. The engagement was short and permanently ended the threat. According to ancient accounts, the victory was achieved with relatively light casualties on the Roman side, though such figures should always be treated with caution.

It was after Zela that Caesar reportedly uttered the phrase, "Veni, vidi, vici"—"I came, I saw, I conquered." The line was preserved by Suetonius. After Pharnaces died, Caesar recognized Mithridates of Pergamum with territory in the region.

The situation in Italy had deteriorated while Caesar was on campaign. Mark Antony was managing affairs as Caesar's deputy, with Lepidus holding authority in Rome itself. The debt crisis had been building throughout the civil war. Years of disruption and uncertainty had strained Italy's economy, and now the tension erupted into street violence. Antony moved to suppress it but was delayed by a mutiny among some of Caesar's legions. Clashes broke out in the Forum between his men and those of Publius Cornelius Dolabella, a political opponent.

By the time Caesar landed in Italy, he found a city in disorder. He moved quickly. He relieved Antony of his responsibilities—Antony was a capable soldier but had proven an unreliable administrator—and turned his attention to the mutinous troops.

Caesar's handling of the mutiny became one of the most celebrated episodes of his career. He assembled the men, addressed them as "civilians," and dismissed them from service. The word "civilian" was a calculated insult. For Roman soldiers, whose sense of honor and identity were inseparable from their status as legionaries, it struck at the core of who they were. The men broke. They begged to be readmitted and handed over the ringleaders themselves. Caesar accepted them back after a deliberate show of hesitation. The mutiny collapsed. Caesar also moved to defuse the debt agitation politically, finding offices for some of those involved, including Dolabella. Rome had been pacified.

Caesar had little time to consolidate his gains. The Pompeians (which we call Republicans moving onward) in Africa had formalized their alliance with King Juba of Numidia and assembled a substantial force. In Spain, Caesar's governor had been overthrown, and the Republicans had regained control of the provinces, which led to more manpower and valuable mines. Caesar placed Lepidus in charge of Italy, raised new funds, assembled a large army, and sailed for Africa in 46 BCE. It was the more immediate threat, and he intended to deal with it first.

Chapter 6: Final Campaigns and Return to Rome

The Bloodshed Continues

Caesar landed in Africa in December 47 BCE with an advance force, waiting for the bulk of his army to cross from Italy. He eventually assembled roughly thirty thousand men, but in the early weeks, he was operating with far fewer men, and he was in a vulnerable position. The Republicans harassed him while he waited for reinforcements.

Ancient sources report that Caesar elevated a minor member of the Scipio family to his staff during this period, possibly to counter a widespread belief among ordinary soldiers that no Scipio could be defeated in Africa. This superstition was rooted in the memory of Scipio Africanus and the Second Punic War. This may have been deliberate propaganda or just a way to boost morale.

The Republican force was formidable. It was commanded by Quintus Caecilius Metellus Pius Scipio, with Titus Labienus, once one of Caesar's finest lieutenants in the Gallic campaigns, directing their army in the field. Their alliance with Juba of Numidia gave them a large force of elite Numidian cavalry, which would prove to be a persistent problem for Caesar's infantry-heavy army.

Caesar had secured an alliance with the Kingdom of Mauretania, whose forces raided Numidia and prevented Juba from committing his full strength against the Caesarians. Republican supply lines to Rome were not secure either. A small Republican naval force was operating in the central Mediterranean, which threatened Caesar's own communications. The Republican command structure was also divided among several leaders, which may have complicated coordination. Cato the Younger was present in Africa and exerted strong political influence within the leadership. It was, to put it lightly, an uneasy coalition.

Caesar's full force did not assemble until January 46 BCE. In the meantime, he moved against local towns to secure his position and gather supplies. Once, after taking a small settlement, his force was returning to their base at Ruspina (in modern Tunisia) when Labienus appeared with a largely cavalry-based army and moved to surround them. Caesar's men were mostly heavy infantry. These were battle-hardened and disciplined men, but they lacked the mobility to simply outrun encirclement. Caesar extended his lines to prevent being outflanked. Labienus, who knew Caesar's tactics very well, extended his own lines to take advantage of his numerical superiority. The Numidian horsemen began circling and throwing javelins into the Roman formation. It was starting to look like this would not end well for Caesar.

However, Caesar kept his nerve. Later sources claim he personally intervened when an eagle standard bearer began to fall back, seizing the standard himself and turning it to face the enemy, though this account is likely an embellishment. What is clear is that the Caesarian line held. Caesar ordered his men to charge forward and throw their javelins as they closed in on the enemy. The sudden aggression disrupted Labienus's formation and created enough chaos for Caesar to disengage. He withdrew his force to Ruspina and fortified the camp.

This engagement was not a victory. It was at best a successful withdrawal after near-encirclement, and it exposed how vulnerable Caesar's force was until his full army arrived.

Bust of middle-aged Julius Caesar.[18]

Victory in Africa

Thankfully for Caesar, the Republican commanders adopted a cautious strategy that bought him the time he needed. They had good reasons to avoid immediate battle. Their Numidian cavalry gave them a significant advantage in open country, and they believed that Caesar's supplies would deteriorate the longer the campaign dragged on. A weakened Caesar, they hoped, would be easier to destroy or force into surrender.

Political pressure within the Republican leadership complicated this. Cato the Younger, for instance, pushed for more aggressive action, arguing that delay helped Caesar more than it helped them. Eventually, the Republicans moved toward a more offensive posture. It gave Caesar the battle he had been waiting for.

The African campaign is documented primarily in the *De Bello Africo*, which is part of the Caesarian body of writings, although it was almost certainly not written by Caesar himself. The author remains unknown. It is a valuable source, though like all ancient military accounts, it should be read with caution.

The two armies met at Thapsus on what most sources place in April 46 BCE, though some scholars give a February date due to calendar conversion issues between the Julian and older Roman calendars. The battlefield was a narrow corridor of low-lying ground with the sea on one side and a lake and marsh on the other. This terrain neutralized much of the Republican cavalry advantage by removing the open ground Numidian horsemen needed to encircle and harass an enemy force—the same tactic that had nearly destroyed Caesar at Ruspina.

Caesar had anticipated the Republicans' reliance on war elephants and drilled his men specifically in how to counter them. He placed his most experienced legions in the positions most likely to face the elephants and stationed his archers and slingers to target them. When the battle began, he ordered the missile troops forward against the animals. The elephants panicked and stampeded back into the Republican lines, causing chaos. Caesar's cavalry then moved against the enemy camp. The besieged garrison at Thapsus made a sortie but was driven back. Metellus Scipio could not hold his formation together as the left wing began to break. Juba's forces abandoned the field once it was clear the Republicans would be defeated.

What followed the battle was ugly. Caesar's soldiers massacred large numbers of prisoners. Ancient sources report that Caesar ordered them to stop, but he could not get them to listen.

The Battle of Thapsus destroyed the main Republican army in Africa. Metellus Scipio fled but did not escape; he was cornered at sea and killed himself rather than surrender. Juba and Marcus Petreius were trapped and chose death on their own terms, fighting a duel whose outcome ancient sources describe differently, with the survivor killed by a slave. Cato the Younger, the political backbone of the Republican cause, retreated to Utica and took his own life rather than accept Caesar's mercy.

With their army destroyed and their leading figures dead or dying, organized Republican resistance had effectively collapsed. Spain was still an issue, as Republican commanders still held significant territory and manpower there. But the war's center of gravity had shifted decisively. Caesar had broken the Republican cause in Africa.

Forces under Publius Sittius, operating alongside Caesar's Mauretanian allies, defeated elements of Juba's army and cut off escape routes. Caesar moved through the province imposing financial penalties on communities and individuals who had supported his enemies. Roman commanders financed their campaigns through a combination of state resources, booty, loans, and confiscation, and Caesar needed funds to pay his army and to consolidate his political position. He then annexed part of Numidia, turning it into the new province of Africa Nova, and granted territory to his Mauretanian allies.

Ancient sources, including Suetonius, report a rumor that Caesar had an affair with Eunoë, the wife of the Mauretanian king Bogud. This ancient rumor is impossible to verify, but it surely didn't help Caesar's reputation as a womanizer.

To Italy!

Once Caesar had arranged affairs to his satisfaction in Africa, he returned to Rome. He was greeted by supporters and sycophants eager for his favor.

Caesar increasingly controlled the electoral process, often directly appointing magistrates rather than leaving elections to run their traditional course. Those who had opposed him, such as Cicero, appeared publicly accepting of his rule. In private letters, Cicero lamented the loss of Republican liberty.

The Roman public cheered, though. In September 46 BCE, Caesar celebrated four triumphs: one for Gaul, one for Egypt, one for Pontus, and one for Africa. The triumph was a ritual through which the Senate formally recognized a commander's victory and paraded his conquests before the Roman people. Caesar now turned that Republican institution to his own purposes. All of his major campaigns had involved the defeat of Roman citizens as well as foreign enemies, but the triumphs presented only foreign victories. The Gauls, Egyptians, Pontic forces, and Africans were the enemies on display. The civil war was quietly set aside. It was a careful piece of political theater that recast one man's seizure of power as the expansion of Rome. Each triumph reinforced the image of Caesar not merely as victor in a civil war but as conqueror of the world. Caesar wanted to normalize something that the Roman Republic had no precedent for—a single man who had defeated everyone.

The constitutional reality was also unprecedented. In 46 BCE, Caesar was appointed dictator for ten years, under the title dictator rei publicae constituendae (dictator for the purpose of settling the constitution), the same title Sulla had used. He also held the consulship repeatedly and earned a range of other honors and powers that collectively placed him beyond any check of the Republican system. In public after 46 BCE, he was attended by seventy-two lictors (a bodyguard)—twenty-four for each dictatorship he held simultaneously. A consul would normally receive twelve lictors. Caesar had symbols too. A golden chair, a purple robe, and a statue placed among those of the kings of Rome all helped to build his image. He could defend why he earned each honor, but this power grab was becoming alarming. Elite resentment grew quietly, and conspiratorial networks began to form.

Cleopatra visited Rome again during this period, staying at Caesar's villa across the Tiber with Ptolemy XIV. Cicero, who visited her there, found her arrogant. On September 26th, 46 BCE, the final day of his triumph, Caesar dedicated the Temple of Venus Genetrix in his new Forum. Inside stood a golden statue of Cleopatra. It was a striking gesture, as Cleopatra was both foreign and still alive. It seemed as if Caesar was associating the mother of his child with the divine ancestry of his own family line.

Caesar did not divorce Calpurnia despite having no children with her and despite his affair with Cleopatra. Her family was powerful and well connected. Whether he genuinely respected and loved her is impossible to know. Roman elite men were not expected to be sexually faithful in the modern sense, and Caesar's affairs were notorious enough to feature in his soldiers' marching songs.

Caesar also began to show particular favor to his grand-nephew Octavian, grandson of his beloved sister. Octavian had already been in Caesar's orbit for some time. He saw something in the young man that others, put off by his slight build and fragile health, apparently missed.

A bust of Caesarion.[14]

Caesar's Last Battles

The civil war was not over. The sons of Pompey the Great, Gnaeus and Sextus, had assumed leadership of the Republican cause and seized control of most of Roman Iberia, exploiting the incompetence and greed of the governor Caesar had appointed there. Labienus, who had survived Thapsus, joined them and used his considerable military talent to assemble a large force. Ancient sources claim there were up to thirteen legions, though many were newly raised rather than veteran formations.

Pompey the Great had commanded in Spain for years and built deep networks of loyalty among local elites, veteran soldiers, and provincial communities. Those ties had passed to his sons. The peninsula had strong recruitment potential, experienced local fighters who had absorbed Roman military discipline, and enormous resources in mining wealth. It was also geographically distant from Rome, which meant it would be difficult to reinforce quickly and easy to hold against a cautious enemy.

Caesar had suppressed Spain in 49 BCE, but Pompeian roots ran deeper there than a single campaign could destroy. If Gnaeus and Sextus could consolidate their position, they would control the western half of the Roman world. The situation was serious enough that Caesar left Italy in November 46 BCE with limited forces that would be reinforced by additional legions upon their arrival. He made the journey to Spain with extraordinary speed, impressing his contemporaries.

Caesar summoned his grand-nephew Octavian to join him during the campaign, an early sign of his favor. However, Octavian did not reach him due to illness.

Caesar began operations in southern Spain in early 45 BCE. He relieved the Republican siege of Ulia and moved on Córdoba, one of the most important cities in the peninsula. The fighting was brutal. Both sides committed atrocities and gave little quarter.

Gnaeus, following Labienus's counsel, refused to be drawn into open battle. He shadowed Caesar's legions through the winter, believing that Caesar's army would be worn down by cold, disease, and supply problems. Caesar responded by moving suddenly on Ategua and besieging it. The Republican commander executed deserters, but the city fell in February 45 BCE.

The fall of Ategua unsettled Gnaeus. His own men were growing restive, and desertions were increasing. He could no longer delay. His larger army was struggling to supply itself, and the initiative had shifted.

There was further maneuvering near the River Salsum, which was indecisive. Eventually, both armies finally met on the plain near Munda in southern Spain. What made Munda dangerous for Caesar was not just the terrain or the numbers. Many of his most experienced veterans had retired after years of service. His legions were understrength. The Republican forces included hardened Spanish fighters who had absorbed local combat styles and were fighting on familiar ground. The Republicans held a strong elevated position, and Caesar, outnumbered and attacking uphill, was in a situation that his own tactical principles would have normally argued against.

The battle that followed was unlike anything else in the civil war. Ancient sources describe hours of grinding, inconclusive infantry combat, with both sides holding their ground and neither breaking. At some point, Caesar personally entered the fighting and rallied Legio X on the right flank. Later accounts describe him leading from the front to prevent a collapse, though some of the details may be embellishment. According to Appian, Caesar later said that at previous battles he had fought for victory, but at Munda, he had fought for his life. It was the closest he had come to personal defeat since Dyrrachium.

The breakthrough came when Gnaeus shifted a legion to reinforce his left, weakening his flank in doing so. The Mauretanian cavalry exploited the opening and struck the exposed position. Combined with the pressure of the sustained infantry assault, the Republican line finally gave way. Once it broke, the rout was total. Ancient sources claim around thirty thousand Republican casualties, though this figure sounds inflated and should be treated with caution. Labienus died on the field. Gnaeus fled with what remained of his forces, but he was captured and killed shortly afterward near Lauro.

Sextus Pompeius escaped. He would go on to control Sicily, disrupt the grain supply to Rome, and challenge the Second Triumvirate for years. He would not be fully suppressed until 36 BCE. So, while Munda ended organized Republican resistance on land, it did not end the civil war.

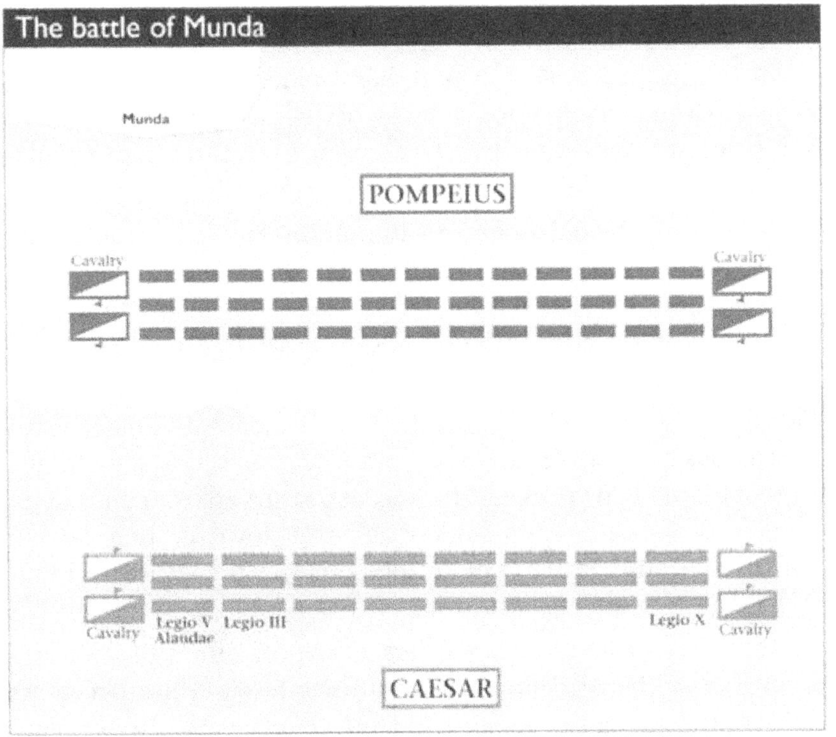

Initial deployment of armies at the Battle of Munda.[15]

Chapter 7: Caesar's Dictatorship and Reforms

Remaking Rome

Munda had ended the military threat. Caesar returned to Rome through southern Gaul, establishing veterans' colonies along the way. He also reconciled with Mark Antony, whom he would later name co-consul. He appointed Brutus as praetor for 44 BCE, a deliberate gesture of inclusion toward someone who had come over from the Republican side.

Back in Rome, he celebrated a triumph for the Spanish campaign. It was controversial. Triumphs traditionally celebrated victories over foreign enemies. This one celebrated the killing of fellow Romans, and many found it distasteful, including men Caesar had pardoned, among them Cicero and Brutus.

The forms of Republican government still existed. The Senate still met. Elections still took place. However, the reality was something else entirely. Caesar had packed the Senate with allies, controlled the electoral process, and commanded an army loyal to him personally rather than to the state. The institutions of the Roman Republic functioned as instruments of his will.

Many senators hated it. They believed that only the Roman Republic could guarantee their freedom and that one all-powerful man—however capable—reduced them to subjects. To men like Cicero, the parallel with the Greek tyrants was obvious. But the most dangerous opponents were not the ones who complained openly. Brutus and Cassius had been pardoned and given offices. They said little, but they were watching for a chance to act.

The honors had accumulated steadily since Pharsalus in 48 BCE. The Senate granted Caesar the title praefectus moribus (prefect of morals), giving him the right to revise the senatorial rolls and fill them with his own men. He was given the power to declare war and make peace, which had traditionally belonged to the popular assemblies. Each victory brought more honors. The Senate granted them eagerly, partly out of loyalty, partly out of fear, and partly because men who wanted his favor understood that honors cost them nothing.

By early 44 BCE, the accumulation of honors had reached its endpoint. Caesar was appointed dictator perpetuo (dictator in perpetuity). There was no time limit for this office and no expectation of resignation. It was a formal break with everything the dictatorship had meant. His first dictatorship in 49 BCE had been brief and constitutionally irregular, though it was formally approved. After that, he held the office three more times. In 46 BCE, he secured it for ten years. Not even during the Second Punic War, when Hannibal was marching through Italy, had the dictatorship been extended to anything like that length.

Caesar the King?

Even those sympathetic to Caesar likely had doubts about his growing power. He wore distinctive purple and triumphal dress on occasions that would previously have been reserved for specific ceremonies. What alarmed observers was not the color itself—Roman magistrates had always used purple in various forms. But Caesar wore it often, and he seemed to have claimed it as his. He sat on a gilded chair. He had his portrait stamped on coins, a practice unknown in Rome but standard among the Hellenistic monarchies of the East.

A denarius of Julius Caesar.[16]

The question of whether Caesar wanted to be king was tested publicly in February 44 BCE at the festival of Lupercalia. Mark Antony, who was participating in the festival, approached Caesar as he sat watching from the Rostra (a large, elevated platform in the Roman Forum) and placed a diadem on his head, saying the people offered it to him. A few in the crowd applauded. Most were silent. Caesar removed it. Antony offered it again. When Caesar set it aside as an offering to Jupiter and declared that Jupiter alone was king of the Romans, the crowd cheered loudly.

Whether the episode was staged or a genuine offer, it revealed that the Roman people were not ready for a king, and Caesar knew it. Earlier that same year, tribunes Marullus and Flavus had removed royal insignia that had been placed on Caesar's statues in the Forum. Caesar had them stripped of their office and expelled from the Senate. As tribunes, they were the traditional defenders of the common people. Punishing them for defending Republican symbols turned public sentiment against him. Some sources report that when members of a crowd greeted him as rex ("king") on the Appian Way, Caesar replied, "I am not Rex, but Caesar," deflecting the title while doing nothing to dismiss the suspicion behind it.

His accumulation of powers resembled those of a monarch, whether or not he intended to assume the title. Some contemporaries, including Suetonius and Plutarch, portrayed him as increasingly arrogant after his victories. He remained seated when the Senate approached him in formal delegations, surrounded himself with flatterers, and was less willing to read public sentiment than he had earlier in his career.

Whether this reflects reality or the bias of sources writing after his death is difficult to say. What is clear is that he antagonized even some of his supporters, men who felt they were his equals and believed they had not received their share of the honors. In Rome, politics was very personal. Dignitas (reputation and the respect of one's peers) was the currency of public life. Caesar's behavior implied that his own stood so far above everyone else's that theirs barely registered.

Open opposition was limited, but there were reasons for this beyond just cowardice. Many senators had died in the civil war. Some aristocratic families had been politically weakened. Many of those who remained owed their positions directly to Caesar; they had been appointed, promoted, or pardoned by him. Refusing to grant him honors would have appeared disloyal in a political culture that rewarded loyalty. To put it simply, the Senate did not just cave. It had to operate within a system Caesar had changed so thoroughly that independent action carried serious risk.

The Senate renamed the month of Quintilis—the month of Caesar's birth—Julius, a name that has endured in the Western calendar for over two millennia. He had already dedicated the Temple of Venus Genetrix, tying his family's claimed descent from Venus to a permanent religious monument at the center of Roman public life. The Julian line traced its ancestry from Venus through Aeneas to his son Iulus. This was not unusual; claims of divine ancestry were common among Roman elites, and they were politically useful, though they were not necessarily taken as literal theology. What made Caesar's use of it different was the scale and the context. Hellenistic monarchs routinely emphasized divine lineage to legitimize their rule. By building a temple, placing Cleopatra's statue inside it, and publicly associating his own family with divine origin, Caesar was using the language of an Eastern monarchy in the heart of the Roman Republic. His opponents noticed.

His veterans remained fiercely loyal. The urban population was more divided. Many still revered him as the man who had ended the civil wars and delivered bread and entertainment, but some sources suggest there was unease among segments of the populace about his concentration of power. After his assassination, Antony's funeral oration unleashed popular fury against the conspirators. The city erupted in violence, and the assassins were driven from Rome. That reaction suggests Caesar still had deep popular support. The conspiracy came not from the streets but from the Senate and from men he had trusted.

The Reforms of Caesar

Caesar was a great general, a gifted writer, and an ambitious reformer. Like Sulla before him, he wanted to end the political instability that had plagued Rome for decades. Throughout his years in power, his reforms touched many areas of Roman political and social life.

Citizenship Reform

Caesar carried out a census prompted by concerns about the decline in the citizen population after years of civil war. Many inhabitants had been claiming the grain dole (grain given to citizens each month for free) when they didn't need it, so he reformed the distribution to ensure it reached those with a legitimate right to it. He imposed limits on prolonged absences from the provinces for senators and members of the elite. He extended citizenship to eligible inhabitants of Gaul and Hispania, rewarding allies and facilitating the integration of those provinces into Roman political structures. Only a small portion of the population gained citizenship through these measures, though; it was predominantly the local elite who entered the citizenry. He also granted citizenship to skilled immigrants, such as doctors, who settled in Italy.

Debt was a serious problem. Years of civil war had left many poorer citizens unable to meet their obligations, and the resulting tensions fed the factionalism that had long destabilized the city. Caesar restructured debt repayment by deducting previously paid interest from the principal owed and by allowing property to be valued at pre-war rates rather than the deflated values produced by the conflict. He also introduced limits on interest rates. These measures protected debtors without simply wiping out what creditors were owed.

Infrastructure Projects

Caesar was a builder on a large scale. His infrastructure projects served two purposes. It would help the urban poor by stimulating the economy. These projects would also serve as a visible legitimization of his rule. He ordered roads built across Italy, often at his own expense. He expanded the Roman Forum by constructing the Forum Iulium (Forum of Caesar). The Temple of Venus Genetrix stood at its center. He improved drainage and urban planning in Rome and undertook several other development projects.

He also ordered the refounding of Carthage and Corinth—both of which had been destroyed by Rome in the previous century—and resettled large numbers of the urban poor in these new colonies. Both became important urban centers in the Roman world.

These projects were funded through war spoils, state revenues, and taxes from the provinces. That is the other side of Roman development. The wealth that built the roads and forums was often extracted from the provinces, sometimes at considerable cost to the people who lived there. The provinces benefited from Roman infrastructure and stability over time, but the relationship was rarely equal.

Forum of Julius Caesar and Temple of Venus Genitrix.[17]

Reorganization of Government

Caesar's political reforms strengthened his grip on power while also addressing genuine administrative needs. He expanded the Senate from roughly six hundred to perhaps as many as nine hundred members. This provided more magistrates and commanders for a growing empire, but it also packed the Senate with his supporters. He increased the number of quaestors, aediles, and praetors to ensure the administration ran smoothly. Plus, he could use these offices to reward loyal men. He restricted political collegia, the street-level associations that had long been a source of factional violence in Rome. He reorganized the courts and restructured jury pools. Even his opponents acknowledged that he was fair in his legal decisions.

Caesar transformed the dictatorship from a temporary emergency office into a long-term governing position. He made the Urban Prefect and Master of Horse into important administrative roles, giving them authority over Rome and Italy that had previously rested with the Senate. By 44 BCE, he had forced the Senate to grant him the right to designate magistrates for years when he would be absent from the city.

The traditional elite found itself increasingly sidelined. Caesar would occasionally grant brief consulships to supporters, bending convention to reward loyalty. This alarmed many in Rome. Change had always been associated with instability, and Caesar was generating a great deal of it.

Military Reforms

Caesar had watched Pompey's veterans destabilize Roman politics through their demands for land. He avoided the same problem by settling his veterans in colonies outside Italy, namely in Africa, Spain, and Gaul. These settlements helped consolidate Roman control in the provinces and, over time, became important centers of Roman culture in those regions. They were settlements, not standing garrisons, though veterans provided experienced manpower in times of crisis.

Caesar also broadened recruitment. He had always been quick to raise auxiliary units—Gallic and German cavalry in particular—and he increasingly enlisted provincials alongside Romans. This was not a fully systematic reform, but it pointed toward what the imperial army would later become. He promised his soldiers land and substantial rewards, and his generosity to his men was key to the loyalty they showed him throughout his campaigns.

Reform of the Calendar

Caesar remained Pontifex Maximus throughout his dictatorship. The College of Pontiffs was responsible for maintaining the calendar, but years of neglect had left it badly out of alignment with the solar year. Festivals were no longer held at the right time of year. Caesar decided to replace the old lunar calendar with a solar one. He based the reform on the work of Sosigenes, an Alexandrian astronomer, drawing on Egyptian and Hellenistic astronomical calculations that had long established the solar year at 365 and a quarter days. The new Julian calendar introduced a regular year of 365 days and a leap year of 366 days every four years to account for the quarter-day remainder.

To realign the calendar before the new system could begin, Caesar ordained that 46 BCE would last 445 days. The Romans called it the year of confusion. The Julian calendar took effect on January 1ˢ, 45 BCE, and became the official system in the Roman administration. Local calendars lasted in some provinces for cultural reasons, but the Julian calendar quickly replaced the old Roman system. It remained the standard in the Western world for over fifteen centuries.

After returning from the civil wars, Caesar showed little sign of slowing down. He enjoyed himself. He had affairs, drank, and lived like a wealthy Roman aristocrat. But he also worked constantly.

His behavior became increasingly high-handed. Those who disagreed with him grew cautious about saying so. Caesar had lived through decades of political violence and had survived too much to think he was still vulnerable. That belief may have cost him his life.

Chapter 8: Assassination and Aftermath

Growing Dangers

By 44 BCE, Caesar faced no open military opposition, though political resentment remained among some of the elite. He was busy implementing reforms and preparing for new campaigns. Several ancient sources portray him as increasingly dismissive of senatorial protocol and less attentive to the political mood than he had been earlier in his career.

A small group of senators began to conspire against him. Cassius Longinus, an able soldier and politician, was one of the instigators. He was alarmed by Caesar's accumulation of power and believed action was necessary before Caesar left Rome on campaign. Caesar was preparing a large-scale Eastern campaign, first against the Dacians north of the Danube, then against the Parthian Empire. The Parthian campaign, in particular, was very ambitious. It was widely seen as an attempt to avenge the catastrophic Roman defeat at Carrhae in 53 BCE, where Crassus and his army had been destroyed. Caesar planned a multi-year expedition that would take him deep into the East. Rome would be left under the control of his deputies, men like Antony and Lepidus, for an indefinite period. For the conspirators, this was the closing of a window. Once Caesar left, the opportunity to act would be gone for years, and his lieutenants would tighten their grip on the city in his absence.

Cassius recruited his brother-in-law, Marcus Brutus. Brutus was a man of principle who had fought with Pompey against Caesar because he was a Republican, even though Pompey had murdered his father.

Caesar had pardoned him after the Battle of Pharsalus and shown him considerable favor. Rumor was that Brutus was Caesar's illegitimate son, though this is unverifiable. He was also said to be descended from the Brutus who had expelled the kings of Rome centuries earlier. This lineage must have weighed heavily on him. He joined the conspiracy despite his personal connection to Caesar, apparently convinced that the Roman Republic needed Caesar to be gone.

The conspirators recruited carefully. Eventually, more than sixty senators were involved. Not all of them were ideological Republicans acting on principle. Some had personal grievances. These were men who felt passed over for honors, sidelined by Caesar's patronage networks, or humiliated by his dominance. Cassius himself was driven partly by genuine Republican conviction and partly by wounded pride.

The mix of motives made the group politically disunited. They had a plan to kill Caesar, but they had no plan for what came after. There was no agreement on how to restore the Roman Republic, no strategy for dealing with Caesar's veterans, and no preparation for the Roman people's reaction.

They debated whether to kill Mark Antony alongside Caesar. Brutus argued against it. Killing only Caesar would make the act look like tyrannicide rather than a coup, which might prevent a new civil war. The others accepted this reluctantly. It proved to be a serious miscalculation. Since Antony survived, he controlled Caesar's papers and funds, and within days, he had turned the city against them.

By March 44 BCE, the conspirators knew they had to move. The Senate meeting of March 15th—the Ides of March, just a normal day in the Roman calendar that would become famous—was their opportunity. Caesar had no formal bodyguard. He was normally surrounded by friends and clients, but in the Senate, he was much more accessible.

At least one ancient source records that a soothsayer warned him his life was in danger on the Ides of March. Caesar is said to have ignored the warning. He may have known conspiracies were being discussed but doubted anyone would act. He had survived so much. He probably believed he was untouchable.

The Most Famous Assassination in History

The Senate was to meet in the Curia of Pompey within the Theatre of Pompey complex. The traditional Senate house had been destroyed in 52 BCE and was still being rebuilt. Caesar was delayed. His wife

Calpurnia had dreamed of his bloodied corpse and begged him not to go. He initially agreed to cancel. Then, Decimus Brutus, one of the conspirators, arrived at the house and persuaded him otherwise, arguing it would look weak to stay home because of a bad dream. Caesar finally relented.

On his way to the Theatre of Pompey, he passed the soothsayer who had supposedly warned him about the Ides of March. According to later sources, Caesar remarked that the Ides of March had come. The soothsayer replied that they had not yet passed. Caesar went to the Senate meeting anyway.

He entered without a bodyguard—he had dismissed his Spanish guard months earlier—which made him vulnerable once inside the chamber. One of the conspirators detained Mark Antony outside, as the conspirators were aware of his formidable reputation as a soldier. Inside, roughly two hundred senators were present for what appeared to be a routine formal meeting. Around sixty of them were conspirators.

Caesar took his seat. The assassins positioned themselves around him under the pretense of joining a group petition. It was carefully staged. Lucius Tillius Cimber stepped forward first, drawing Caesar's attention with a request. Cimber then seized Caesar's toga, which was the prearranged signal for the attack. It was also a way to restrain him.

Casca struck first, stabbing Caesar in the neck. The wound was not immediately fatal. Caesar grabbed Casca's arm. According to Plutarch, he cried out, "Casca, you villain, what are you doing?" He tried to fight back, but the rest closed in. The conspirators attacked him with concealed daggers. He was stabbed twenty-three times. Some ancient sources claim that when Caesar saw Brutus among the attackers, he said in Greek, "Kai su, teknon?" ("You too, child?"). Others report he said nothing. The line "Et tu, Brute?" ("And you, Brutus?") is Shakespeare's invention. It has no basis in the ancient sources.

Caesar wrapped his toga around himself as he fell. He died at the base of a statue of Pompey, the man he had defeated in the civil war, whose cause many of the conspirators had once supported. That the most powerful man in the Roman world fell at the feet of his greatest rival, in a building that bore his rival's name, was not lost on contemporaries. The divisions of the Roman Republic had never really been resolved. They had simply been suppressed.

A later medical examination, attributed to a physician named Antistius, concluded that only one of the twenty-three wounds had been fatal. Caesar's body reportedly lay unattended for some time before slaves finally removed it. One of the most consequential figures in the history of the ancient world died on the floor of a meeting room, surrounded by men he had pardoned.

The assassination of Caesar, a painting dated to the late 19th century. [18]

The Aftermath of the Assassination

After the assassination, the conspirators marched through Rome proclaiming that the people were free. The response was not what they had hoped for. The city did not rise to join them. The Romans had lived through decades of political violence and civil war. Most stayed off the streets. The conspirators withdrew to the Capitoline Hill when popular support failed to appear.

In the days that followed, civil war was not yet inevitable. Mark Antony negotiated a compromise in the Senate that temporarily held the city together. The assassins were granted amnesty. At the same time, Caesar's acts, appointments, and legislation were ratified and allowed to stand. It was a careful political balance. The conspirators escaped punishment, but everything Caesar had built remained in place. The arrangement suited Antony. It gave him legal continuity over Caesar's affairs while leaving the conspirators without a clear path to dismantling his legacy. For a brief moment, an uneasy peace held.

But it did not last. Caesar's funeral destroyed it. Antony delivered the eulogy and used the occasion to promote his own agenda. He displayed Caesar's bloodstained toga to the crowd, holding it up so the wounds were visible. According to some ancient sources, a wax effigy showing Caesar's twenty-three wounds was on display. Antony read the will aloud, including Caesar's gifts to the Roman people and the gardens he left for public use.

The crowd's grief turned to fury. The body was burned spontaneously in the Forum, the crowd feeding the pyre with whatever came to hand. Rioters attacked the houses of the conspirators. The city that had stood back in cautious silence days earlier had turned. The assassins had badly misjudged how deeply Caesar was beloved in the city.

Octavian, Caesar's eighteen-year-old great-nephew, was not in Rome at the time of the assassination. He was in Apollonia on the Adriatic coast, preparing to join Caesar's Parthian campaign. Once Caesar's will was read, his status as adopted heir became known quickly. Leading figures in the city took note. Antony, who was serving as consul at the time of Caesar's death, had emerged as the dominant Caesarian in Rome. He controlled Caesar's papers and funds. However, Octavian's claim to Caesar's name and legacy would prove more powerful than Antony anticipated.

Antony, as executor of Caesar's will, withheld much of Caesar's inheritance from Octavian. Octavian did not accept this quietly. He was young and had a reputation for poor health, but he was intelligent, patient, and utterly ruthless. He borrowed heavily to honor Caesar's favors to the Roman people out of his own funds, which earned him a lot of goodwill among Caesar's veterans and the urban poor. He flattered Cicero, who hoped to use him as a tool against Antony, and cultivated allies among the senators who had stayed out of the conspiracy.

Antony, meanwhile, overreached. He moved to seize the province of Cisalpine Gaul, which the conspirator Decimus Brutus was holding. The Senate declared this illegal and dispatched the two consuls of 43 BCE, Aulus Hirtius and Gaius Vibius Pansa, along with Octavian and his legions of Caesar's veterans, to oppose him. At the Battle of Mutina in 43 BCE, Antony was defeated. Both consuls died in the fighting. Ancient sources noted the convenience of their deaths, though no firm evidence of foul play exists. Octavian found himself in command of the Senate's forces, as well as his own.

He did not use that position to serve the Senate. He turned his army around and made peace with Antony. He understood that the Senate regarded him as a useful instrument, not a partner, and that Caesar's enemies were his enemies too. Together with Antony and the veteran Caesarian Lepidus, Octavian formed the Second Triumvirate in 43 BCE. Unlike the informal alliance between Caesar, Pompey, and Crassus a generation earlier, this was a legally constituted arrangement. The Lex Titia formally granted the three men extraordinary powers for five years. They had the power to make laws, appoint magistrates, and govern the Roman world between them. It was as if the Roman Republic's constitution had been suspended.

The proscriptions that followed were savage and systematic. Ancient sources give varying figures, but around three hundred senators and two thousand equestrians were targeted. The proscriptions served two purposes—political and financial. Enemies were eliminated. Their confiscated property and estates funded the triumvirs' armies. Lists of names were posted publicly. Men were dragged from their homes and killed in the street, in their gardens, and in temples where they sought refuge. Slaves who betrayed their masters were rewarded. Sons informed on their fathers.

Cicero was among the victims. Antony had never forgiven him for the Philippics, the speeches attacking him after Caesar's death. Cicero was caught trying to flee Italy and was executed. His head and hands were brought to Antony and displayed in the Forum. Later sources, including Cassius Dio, report that Fulvia, Antony's wife, drove a pin through the severed tongue in mockery of his oratory, though this detail is likely an embellishment.

The confiscations were brutal but also effective. The triumvirs raised the forces they needed. The leading conspirators had already departed Rome. Brutus and Cassius moved east, raising forces in Macedonia and Asia Minor by levying heavy taxes and requisitions on the eastern provinces.

The conspirators had an army, but the assassination had already failed in every way that mattered. The conspirators had killed Caesar with no plan for what came next. They had not secured the loyalty of the legions. They had not controlled the public reaction. They had left Antony alive and free to act. They had dismissed Octavian as a sickly teenager with no political weight. Every one of those miscalculations would cost them. The Roman Republic they thought they were saving would not survive another decade. The men who killed Caesar in the name of liberty had set in motion the final destruction of everything they claimed to be defending.

Avenging Caesar

Mark Antony and Octavian led their armies eastward, proclaiming they would avenge Caesar's murder. They met the forces of the Liberators (those who had "liberated" Rome from tyranny) at Philippi in Macedonia in 42 BCE. Octavian was seriously ill during much of the campaign; as we noted before, his health had always been fragile. So, Antony took effective command of their forces.

The first engagement was tactically mixed. Antony defeated Cassius on one flank, while Brutus overran Octavian's position on the other. Cassius, unaware that Brutus had succeeded, received false reports of a general defeat and took his own life. It was a huge loss for the Liberators. Cassius was widely regarded as the more capable military commander of the two, and his death weakened their position considerably.

After weeks of maneuvering, the two sides met again. At the Second Battle of Philippi, the combined forces of Antony and Octavian defeated Brutus. His army collapsed, and Brutus committed suicide rather than be taken. The last serious military opposition to the Caesarian cause was finished.

A painting of the Battle of Philippi.[19]

The victory at Philippi settled who controlled the Roman world, but it did not settle who would dominate it. The division of territory that followed contained the seeds of a future conflict. Antony took the wealthy Eastern provinces—Egypt, Syria, and Asia Minor—where the tax revenues were enormous, and the resources of the Hellenistic world were within reach. Octavian was given Italy and the Western provinces—Gaul and Spain. On paper, this looked like an equal split. In practice, Antony had the richer share, and Octavian had the harder task. Italy was the political heart of Rome, but it was also where hundreds of thousands of veterans needed land. Settling them meant confiscating farms from existing owners, which caused bitterness and unrest. Antony could pursue glory in the East largely free of these pressures. Octavian had to manage a resentful Italy with limited funds and no military prestige to speak of.

The Second Triumvirate was renewed by the Treaty of Tarentum in 37 BCE, extending the arrangement for another five years, but the underlying competition for dominance was already pulling the two men apart. Antony emerged as the senior partner in the alliance after Philippi. As part of the political settlement, Octavian's sister, Octavia, married Antony, binding the alliance with a family tie.

Octavian's most pressing external threat was Sextus Pompey. The youngest son of Pompey the Great had seized Sicily and built a powerful fleet while the triumvirs were occupied with the Liberators. Sicily controlled the sea lanes that carried grain from Egypt and Africa to Rome. Sextus understood this. His fleet blockaded the Italian coast and intercepted grain shipments. By 39 BCE, his stranglehold had brought Italy close to famine. Grain shortages in Rome caused riots. The people's anger was directed toward Octavian, who was responsible for Italy and could not protect its food supply. The situation became so dangerous that the triumvirs were forced to negotiate. In the Pact of Misenum in 39 BCE, Octavian and Antony recognized Sextus's control of Sicily, Sardinia, Corsica, and the Peloponnese and promised him future political honors in exchange for his ending the blockade and allowing grain ships to pass. It was a humiliating concession, driven entirely by the threat of popular revolt in Rome.

The peace did not hold. Sextus and the triumvirs soon accused each other of violating the terms, and hostilities resumed. Octavian suffered serious naval setbacks in 38 BCE when his own attempts to dislodge Sextus failed badly. It was Agrippa, Octavian's most capable general, who solved the problem. He spent time building and training an entirely new fleet from scratch at Lake Avernus. At the naval Battle of Naulochus in 36 BCE, fought off the coast of Sicily, Agrippa destroyed Sextus's fleet. Sextus fled east and was later captured and killed. The defeat of Sextus transformed Octavian's position in the West. The grain supply was restored, the unrest in Rome ended, and his popularity recovered.

In the aftermath of Naulochus, Lepidus attempted to claim Sicily for himself, bringing his African legions and challenging Octavian's authority. Octavian outmaneuvered him politically—his soldiers defected rather than fight Caesar's heir—and stripped him of any real power. Lepidus had held the title of Pontifex Maximus since 44 BCE. Octavian allowed him to keep the title but exiled him from public life. He spent the remaining decades of his life under house arrest at Circeii. His removal was the end of the Second Triumvirate in any meaningful sense. The Roman world was now divided between two men.

The divide was not just territorial. It was becoming increasingly ideological. Antony spent more and more time in the East, drawn into the orbit of Cleopatra and the Hellenistic monarchies. He adopted Eastern dress and customs, distributed Roman territories to Cleopatra's children, and presented himself in ways that reflected the god Dionysus. Octavian watched all of this carefully and made sure Rome watched too. He positioned himself as the defender of Roman tradition, Italian values, and Republican custom. Propaganda began shaping the conflict before a single battle was fought. By the time the two men moved toward open war, Octavian had already won the battle in Rome.

Mark Antony and Cleopatra

After Philippi, Antony turned his attention to the East. He met Cleopatra at Tarsus in 41 BCE. Their alliance was as much political as personal. Antony needed Egypt's wealth and resources for his Eastern ambitions. Cleopatra needed Roman military power to secure her dynasty. The relationship served both of them.

In 40 BCE, Cleopatra gave birth to twins by Antony. A third child followed several years later.

Antony reorganized the Eastern provinces and launched a major invasion of Parthia in 36 BCE, partly to avenge Crassus and partly to rival the achievements of Alexander the Great. It failed badly. His army suffered serious losses, and he was forced into a costly retreat. The Parthian campaign damaged both his reputation and his military strength at a critical moment.

Meanwhile, Octavian was building his position in the West and conducting a propaganda campaign against his rival. In 32 BCE, he allegedly obtained Antony's will from the Vestal Virgins, whether legally or not, and read it aloud in the Senate. The will reportedly requested that Antony be buried in Alexandria alongside Cleopatra, suggesting he intended to shift the center of Roman power to Egypt. Octavian ensured this circulated widely. He framed the coming conflict not as another Roman civil war—the public had no appetite for more of those—but as a war between Rome and a foreign queen who had seduced a Roman commander away from his duties and his people. Cleopatra was portrayed as a dangerous Eastern temptress who had corrupted Antony and threatened to make Rome subservient to Egypt. Antony was not cast as a Roman rebel but as her instrument. It was skillful and deliberately constructed. Octavian understood that legitimacy mattered as much as an army did.

In 35 BCE, after the failure of his Parthian campaign, Octavia traveled to the East with money, troops, and supplies to support her husband. She reached Athens. Antony ordered her not to proceed further and refused to receive her. She returned to Rome.

In 34 BCE, Antony held the Donations of Alexandria, a public ceremony in which he and Cleopatra distributed territories across the East. Cleopatra was declared Queen of Kings, and her son Caesarion, by Caesar, was declared King of Kings. Her children with Antony received other Eastern territories. Some of these lands were Roman client kingdoms. The event was seen in Rome as Antony handing Roman possessions to a foreign queen and her children. It may have been intended partly as political theater to impress Eastern audiences, but in Rome, it played directly into Octavian's hands.

By 33 BCE, the Second Triumvirate had expired. Antony refused to relinquish his command. He had been designated consul for 31 BCE, but the escalating conflict made taking office impossible. Several of his allies and supporters defected as his position weakened. In 32 BCE, Antony formally divorced Octavia, Octavian's sister. By then, he was living openly with Cleopatra in Alexandria. The divorce gave Octavian a clear political advantage. Antony could now be portrayed not simply as a rival but as a Roman leader who had abandoned his Roman wife for a foreign queen.

That year, the Senate, acting under Octavian's influence, declared war on Cleopatra. Antony was stripped of his powers. Octavian had framed the conflict carefully. This was a war against a foreign queen, not a Roman civil war, and Antony was cast as her consort rather than as Rome's enemy.

Antony and Cleopatra assembled a large fleet and army in Greece, preparing for what appeared to be an invasion of Italy. Agrippa, Octavian's trusted general, moved first. He captured key ports along the Greek coast and strangled Antony's supply lines. Antony's forces began to suffer from the lack of food and from disease throughout the summer. His land army remained large on paper, but its fighting effectiveness declined.

In September 31 BCE, at Actium on the western coast of Greece, Antony attempted to break out of Octavian's naval blockade with his fleet. Agrippa outmaneuvered him. During the battle, Cleopatra withdrew with her squadron; whether this was a planned escape or a breakdown in coordination is debated by ancient sources and modern historians alike. Antony followed her. The bulk of his fleet was destroyed or surrendered. His land army, abandoned and leaderless, surrendered shortly afterward.

But Actium did not end the war immediately. Antony and Cleopatra still controlled Egypt, and Octavian spent the following year consolidating his victory before advancing on Alexandria.

Octavian marched on Egypt in 30 BCE. Antony's remaining forces melted away, and he eventually took his own life. Cleopatra, reportedly unwilling to be displayed in Octavian's triumph, did the same. Ancient sources describe her dying from a snakebite, though the exact circumstances are uncertain.

The conquest of Egypt was not simply a military victory. Octavian took the country as his personal domain rather than making it a standard Roman province. Its enormous agricultural wealth and the revenue flowing from its trade became his own private treasury. He banned senators from entering Egypt without his permission, ensuring that no rival could use its riches as a base for challenging him. The wealth of Egypt funded his armies, his building programs, and the political settlement that would follow. It was one of the foundations on which his dominance of Rome was built.

Caesarion, Cleopatra's son by Caesar and perhaps the only biological child of Julius Caesar, was executed after the conquest, almost certainly on Octavian's orders. He was a potential rival claimant to Caesar's legacy, after all. With Caesarion dead, no serious rival remained.

The Roman Republic was effectively dead. This was not simply the result of one man's ambition. The system had been failing for generations. The Senate had grown dependent on powerful individuals to manage a vast empire that its institutions were never designed to control. Armies had become loyal to their generals rather than to the state, a process that Caesar and those before him had accelerated. Extraordinary commands had been granted so routinely that they had become normal. After a century of political violence, assassination, and civil war, most Romans had stopped believing that the old order could deliver the stability they needed.

Octavian understood this. He preserved the forms of Republican government—the Senate, the magistracies, and the elections—while concentrating real power in his own hands. Within a few years, he would take the name Augustus and become Rome's first emperor, though he was careful never to call himself king. The Roman Republic had not been abolished. It had simply been made irrelevant.

Chapter 9: The Legacy of Julius Caesar

Caesar and the Death of the Roman Republic

Caesar was one of the most important figures in Western history. His campaigns, strategies, reforms, and writings left a mark on Rome and on Western civilization that can still be felt today. That legacy is complex and difficult to summarize.

When Caesar crossed the Rubicon, he triggered a civil war that engulfed the Mediterranean for years and dealt a severe blow to the Roman Republic, an institution already weakened by decades of internal conflict. He did not set out to destroy it. In the early stages of the conflict, his aim was more limited. He wanted to avoid prosecution by his enemies in the Senate and to retain the extraordinary powers he had earned through his campaigns. He believed this was his right. His victories made that position irreversible. By 45 BCE, he dominated the Roman world.

He made himself dictator, but he was not a conventional tyrant. He did not abolish Republican institutions. He worked through them and around them at the same time, accumulating powers and offices that stripped those institutions of any real independence. He limited the independence of the two consuls, reducing them from chief magistrates of the state to men who functioned within the system he created. He expanded and packed the Senate, weakening the influence of the old aristocratic families and ensuring that the Senate could not act against him. He limited the independence of the tribunes—the traditional champions of the Roman people—though he did not formally abolish the office. He named Octavian as his heir in his will, but he did not create a legal mechanism for hereditary rule. The question of how power would pass after his death was left unresolved.

Still, the damage to the Republican system was nonetheless real and lasting. After his assassination, the old order could not be restored. The conspirators may have wanted that to happen, but the institutions were no longer in place to allow that to happen smoothly.

It should be acknowledged that the Roman Republic was already in serious difficulty before Caesar even crossed the Rubicon. For almost a century, ever since the time of the Gracchi brothers, the state had been shaken by political violence, the rise of military strongmen, and the breakdown of the old order among the senatorial elite. Whether the Roman Republic would have survived without Caesar is a question that cannot be answered with confidence. Some historians argue it was already doomed. Others point out that the idea of the republic remained powerful and that large parts of the Roman elite remained genuinely committed to it. It is possible, though of course not certain, that a victory for the Pompeian cause might have allowed some version of the old government to continue, as Sulla had briefly done after his own civil war. Caesar's victory made that question moot. Too many of the old Republican elite had died. Those who replaced them were willing to work with an autocrat. His victories sealed the transformation, and his system of government, however improvised, paved the way for the imperial order that followed.

Julius Caesar and the Rise of Europe

Caesar is often ranked among the greatest commanders in history, alongside Alexander the Great and Genghis Khan. His campaigns extended Roman power into regions that would shape the future of an entire continent. Military academies have studied his tactics and strategies for centuries. Napoleon was one of his most enthusiastic students.

The conquest of Gaul was his most important military achievement. Before it, Rome had been primarily a Mediterranean power. After the defeat of Vercingetorix at Alesia, it became a continental one. The Roman occupation of Gaul—what is now France, Belgium, and parts of Switzerland—unified a fragmented region under a common administrative and cultural system. The Latin language, Roman law, urban infrastructure, and eventually Christianity spread through these territories in the centuries that followed. What long-term shape Gaul might have taken without Roman conquest is impossible to say, but it is fair to say that the foundations of what became French civilization were built on Roman ones.

Caesar also conducted expeditions beyond the Rhine into Germanic territory, crossing the river and displaying Roman power to the tribes on the other side. These were raids rather than conquests. There was no permanent annexation, but Roman contact with the Germanic world had consequences. The cultural exchange between Rome and the Germanic peoples who eventually succeeded Roman power in the West influenced the kingdoms that emerged after Rome's fall. Charlemagne's Frankish empire and the Holy Roman Empire that developed from it drew extensively on Roman models, institutions, and symbols.

Caesar's raids in Britain in 55 and 54 BCE produced no permanent occupation, but they showed that the island could be invaded and that it was worth the effort. Nearly a century later, Emperor Claudius ordered the conquest of Britain in 43 CE. The resulting province of Britannia was Roman for nearly four centuries and left lasting imprints on the island's language, religion, urban geography, and legal traditions. These are long chains of consequence, so it would be an overstatement to lay all of them at Caesar's feet. But his campaigns set many of them in motion.

Julius Caesar and Architecture

Caesar left a visible mark on Rome itself. He built on a large scale, partly to enhance the city's grandeur, partly to stimulate the economy, and partly to associate himself with monuments that would outlast him. His most significant contribution was the Forum Iulium (the Forum of Caesar), which set a new model for civic architecture and inspired the later forums of Augustus and his successors. The Basilica Julia, which he commissioned on the southern edge of the Roman Forum, was a large multi-aisled structure with interior colonnades that became the center of legal and commercial activity in the city. The Temple of Venus Genetrix, which stood at the far end of his Forum, tied divine ancestry to a permanent religious monument at the heart of Rome.

The architectural styles and techniques developed under Caesar and Augustus became the classical template, replicated by Romanized elites across the empire. They later inspired architects from the Renaissance to the modern era. Many of the public buildings, courthouses, and civic institutions of later European and American cities were built in direct imitation of Roman models.

Caesar's Calendar

The calendar Caesar introduced in 45 BCE was one of his most lasting achievements. The reform was the work of Egyptian astronomers working at his direction, notably Sosigenes of Alexandria. It replaced the old Roman calendar, which had drifted badly out of alignment with the solar year, with a system of 365 days and a leap year every 4 years. The new calendar kept Rome's traditional festivals and religious dates in place, which made it easier for people to accept. It was adopted across the empire and remained in use throughout the Western world long after Rome had fallen.

By the late 16th century, the Julian calendar had drifted roughly ten days out of alignment with the solar year, prompting Pope Gregory XIII to commission a reform. The Gregorian calendar, introduced in 1582, removed ten accumulated days and refined the leap-year rule for century years. Britain did not adopt the Gregorian calendar until 1752. Some Orthodox churches continue to use the Julian calendar to this day. The month of July still retains Caesar's name in most major European languages.

Propaganda

Caesar understood that political power required narrative as well as force. His *Commentarii* on the Gallic Wars and on the civil war are classics of Latin prose and remain among the most readable accounts of ancient warfare. They are also works of propaganda. They are written in the third person, presenting Caesar as a figure of cool rationality and consistent success. Mistakes are minimized or reframed as the failures of subordinates or the unreliability of allies. Modern historians treat the *Commentarii* as valuable historical sources while acknowledging their selective and self-serving character. These were not simply private memoirs but public communications. Caesar had them circulated in Rome while he was still on campaign, keeping the Roman public informed—and impressed—with regular accounts of his successes in Gaul. It was a deliberate use of propaganda that had not really been seen before in the Roman world.

His building program served similar purposes. The Temple of Venus Genetrix reinforced his family's claimed divine descent. The Forum

Iulium created a monument in his name at the center of Rome. His mercy toward defeated enemies was itself a form of propaganda, as it was intended to show that his dominance was benevolent rather than tyrannical.

The propaganda methods Caesar developed were absorbed and refined by Augustus, becoming the standard toolkit of Roman imperial ideology. Later European rulers, from medieval kings to early modern monarchs, drew on the same traditions. The idea that a strong ruler legitimizes his power through victory, public works, divine favor, and the language of restoration rather than innovation is, in many ways, a Caesarian inheritance.

The Principate

Caesar's assassination might have ended his political legacy entirely had he not made one crucial decision: naming Octavian as his heir. Octavian lacked Caesar's military genius but proved his equal in political intelligence and considerably his superior in patience and caution. He learned from Caesar's example and perhaps even more from Caesar's mistakes. Caesar had taken power openly and provoked the elite until they killed him. Augustus accumulated the same power gradually, within Republican forms, and died in his bed after forty years of serving as emperor.

The system Augustus built rested on foundations Caesar had laid. The weakening of the Senate's independence, the subordination of the consulship, the control of military patronage, and the use of divine ancestry for political legitimacy were all precedents set by Caesar. Augustus extended citizenship to provincial elites selectively—broad universal citizenship came only in 212 CE under Caracalla—but the process Caesar began of incorporating provincial communities into the Roman political structure continued under his heir and successors. Augustus developed what became the imperial cult, the veneration of the emperor as a divine or semi-divine figure, though in Rome itself, he was careful to present himself as First Citizen rather than a god. He reserved the more explicit divine honors for the Eastern provinces, where such traditions were already established. Official deification came after death, not during life. The ideological claim that a single strong ruler was necessary to protect the people, unify the state, and maintain Rome's greatness was a Caesarian inheritance, developed by Augustus and passed to the emperors who followed.

That system endured in the West until 476 CE and in the East, in the form of the Byzantine Empire, until 1453. Whether it would have developed as it did without Caesar is impossible to say with any certainty. What can be said is that his victories, his methods, his institutions, and his heir shaped the structure of the Roman Empire, and the Roman Empire shaped the world that surrounded it.

Bust of Augustus[90]

The Contested Legacy of Caesar

Caesar was one of the most important figures in the history of the Western world. People who change the course of history tend to be controversial, and Caesar is no exception. His contemporaries were divided on his legacy almost immediately after his death. Cicero condemned him as an enemy of freedom. His supporters revered him as a man who had brought glory, order, and justice to Rome. Augustus carefully cultivated his adopted father's memory and referred to him publicly as his father throughout his reign.

In 42 BCE, the Senate officially deified Caesar, an act that made him Divus Julius (the Divine Julius). He was the first Roman to be formally deified by the state. The timing was politically useful to Augustus, who became the son of a god. Ancient sources report that a comet appeared in the sky during the funeral games held in Caesar's honor shortly after his death. It is known as the Sidus Iulium, or Julian star. Augustus seized on this as evidence of Caesar's divinity and had the comet incorporated into portraits and monuments. A temple to Divus Julius was built in the Roman Forum, on the spot where Caesar's body had been cremated. The cult of the deified Caesar became one of the foundations of the imperial religion that developed under Augustus, and the pattern—a deceased emperor declared divine and his successor ruling as the son of a god—became the template for imperial succession.

Emperors adopted the name Caesar to associate themselves with his legacy. The title passed from ruler to successor across Europe and beyond. In the Germanic world, it became kaiser. In the Slavic world, it became tsar (or czar). Both are direct corruptions of Caesar, used by rulers claiming the legitimacy of the Roman imperial tradition. The word outlived the empire that produced it by more than a millennium. It became synonymous with supreme authority in a way that transcended any specific political system. It was a symbol of power so potent that rulers who had no ethnic or territorial connection to Rome still reached for it.

Russian rulers developed the ideology of Moscow as the Third Rome, claiming inheritance from the Roman imperial system. After the fall of Constantinople in 1453, the Ottoman sultans also claimed to be heirs to the Roman imperial tradition. In Byzantium, the title kaisar evolved into a senior court rank rather than the main imperial title, which became basileus, but it remained in use until the empire's end.

The term Caesarism entered the political vocabulary in the 19th century to describe the rule of one man through military prestige and popular authority, bypassing or subordinating traditional institutions. The French political theorist Auguste Romieu used it in the 1850s to describe Napoleon III's regime, and Napoleon III himself explicitly invoked Caesar as a model and predecessor, commissioning a biography of him and presenting his own rule as a modern version of Caesar's. The idea was that Caesar—and by extension Napoleon—had not destroyed the legitimate government but had rescued a society whose existing institutions could no longer govern. The 19th-century historian Theodor

Mommsen made a version of this argument in his influential history of Rome, portraying Caesar as a great man who recognized that the Roman Republic was finished and acted accordingly. Max Weber later used Caesar as a reference point for his concept of charismatic authority, the idea that certain leaders derive their legitimacy not from tradition or law but from the force of their own personality and the belief of their followers. Whether or not one accepts these ideas, they show that Caesar became something more than a historical figure. He became a political archetype and a name associated with a recurring problem in how societies manage the tension between strong leadership and institutional constraints.

The assessment of Caesar has never been settled because it cannot be. Different eras have found different things in him. To Cicero and the Republicans of his own time, he was a tyrant who destroyed the liberty of the Roman aristocracy. To his own soldiers and the urban poor of Rome, he was a patron, a protector, and a source of glory. To Augustus and the imperial tradition, he was the divine originator of a system that brought peace after a century of chaos. To medieval rulers, he was one example among several of legitimate imperial authority. To Renaissance humanists, he exemplified what Machiavelli called *virtù*—the capacity of an exceptional individual to impose his will on circumstance. To Enlightenment republicans and French revolutionaries, he was the destroyer of the Roman Republic and a warning about the danger of military populism. To 19th-century nationalists and imperialists, he was proof that great men make history. To fascist movements of the 20th century, he was a symbol of strong leadership, national renewal, and contempt for parliamentary weakness. To modern historians attentive to the human cost of conquest, he is the man responsible for the deaths and enslavement of a large number of people in Gaul in a campaign whose scale and methods have led some scholars to apply the word genocide, however contested that term is when applied to the ancient world.

Modern historians debate Caesar without reaching any consensus. Was he a revolutionary or essentially conservative? Was he a man who wanted to preserve Rome's power and his own position within it rather than transform its social order? Did he genuinely seek to create a monarchy, or was he accumulating power pragmatically without a fixed goal in mind? Was the Roman Republic already collapsing before he crossed the Rubicon, making his role more of a catalyst than a cause?

Was he primarily a reformer who saw clearly what Rome needed or an opportunist who used the language of reform to justify his personal ambition? The ancient sources do not resolve these questions, and neither do the modern ones.

What can be said is that the Caesar later ages remembered often reflect the preoccupations of those ages as much as the man himself. The Caesar of the Renaissance is not quite the same figure as the Caesar of the Enlightenment or the Caesar of the 19th century or the Caesar of today. Each generation has reconstructed him in light of its own anxieties about power, liberty, greatness, and violence. That is the fate of figures who genuinely change the world. They become screens onto which later eras project their own questions. Caesar has been a tyrant, a founder, a strategist, a demagogue, a reformer, and a warning. He will probably continue to be all of these things because the questions his life raises—about how power is seized and justified, about what individuals can do to history and what history does to individuals, and about the price of greatness—are not questions that will ever go away.

Conclusion

Caesar's life does not give us any easy conclusions. It never has. He was a priest and a politician before he was a general. He was a reformer and a destroyer at the same time. He used the Republican system to climb to the top and then dismantled the checks that the system depended on. He was capable of extraordinary mercy and extraordinary ruthlessness, sometimes within the same campaign.

This book has traced his career from its beginnings to its consequences. The wars in Gaul and the chaos of the late Roman Republic. The crossing of the Rubicon and the civil wars that followed. The brief dictatorship and the assassination on the Ides of March. The long aftermath—the second round of civil wars, the rise of Augustus, and the transformation of Rome into an empire that endured for centuries in the West and over a millennium in the East.

Along the way, this book has tried to show the man behind the legend. His relationship with Cleopatra, which was as political as it was personal. His genius for warfare and the principles that made him one of the most studied commanders in history. His instinct for propaganda and the ways he shaped his own image. The calendar that still structures our year. The buildings that changed Rome's skyline. The writings that are still read two thousand years after his death.

There are many myths surrounding Caesar, and they are largely his own creation. He wrote his own history, literally. This book has tried to separate what is known from what is claimed and to note where the evidence runs out and interpretation begins.

What emerges is a figure who resists a simple verdict. He was not simply a tyrant, and he was not simply a savior. He was a man of his time who pushed his things past their breaking point. Yes, the Roman Republic was already under enormous strain before Caesar crossed the Rubicon. Whether it would have survived without him is impossible to know. What is known is that it did not survive and that the system Augustus built on the ruins of it shaped the political world of Europe, the Middle East, and beyond for more than a thousand years.

Caesar's name became a title. His methods became a template. His story became a mirror in which later ages saw their own questions about power, liberty, and the cost of greatness reflected back at them.

That is still true today. The tension Caesar embodied, between the needs of a state and the ambitions of individuals, between institutions and the men who claim to serve them, and between order and freedom, has not been resolved. It probably cannot be. Understanding how Rome navigated that tension, and ultimately failed to, is not merely an exercise in ancient history. It is a way of thinking about how power works, how republics weaken, and what is at stake when they do.

Here's another book by Enthralling History that you might like

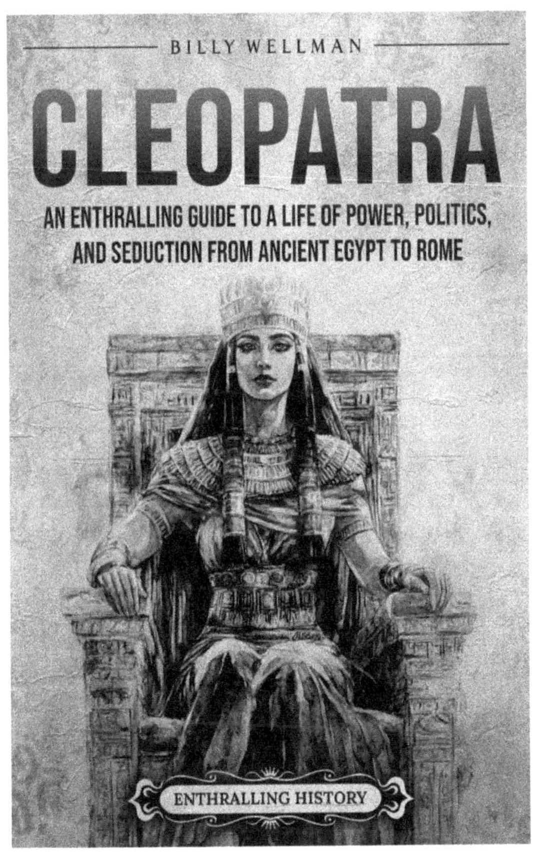

Free limited time bonus

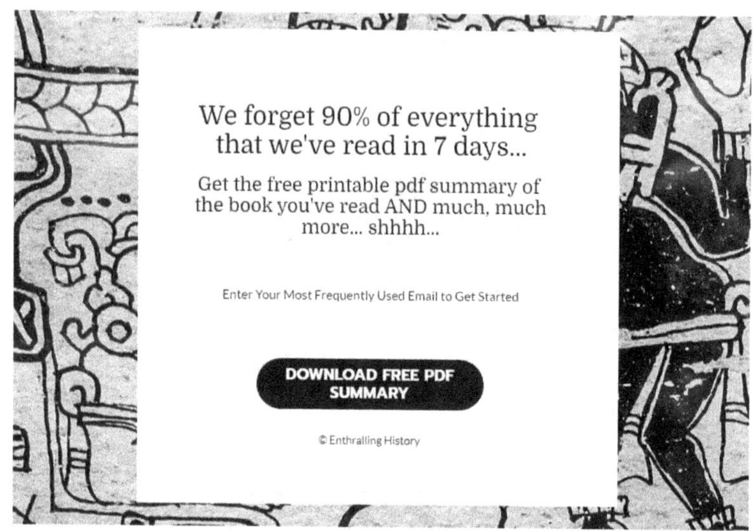

Stop for a moment. We have a free bonus set up for you. The problem is this: we forget 90% of everything that we read after 7 days. Crazy fact, right? Here's the solution: we've created a printable, 1-page pdf summary for this book that you're reading now. All you have to do to get your free pdf summary is to go to the following website:

https://livetolearn.lpages.co/enthrallinghistory/

Or, Scan the QR code!

Once you do, it will be intuitive. Enjoy, and thank you!

Bibliography

Arena, Valentina. *Libertas and the Practice of Politics in the Late Roman Republic.* Cambridge: Cambridge University Press, 2012.

Billows, Richard A. *Julius Caesar: The Colossus of Rome.* New York: Routledge, 2008.

Bradford, Ernle. *Julius Caesar: The Pursuit of Power.* New York: Open Road Media, 2014.

Caesar, Julius. *Commentaries.* London: Penguin, 1985.

Chrissanthos, Stefan G. *The Year of Julius and Caesar: 59 BC and the Transformation of the Roman Republic.* Baltimore: Johns Hopkins University Press, 2019.

Cicero. *Selected Writings.* London: Penguin, 2001.

Goldsworthy, Adrian. *Augustus: From Revolutionary to Emperor.* London: Weidenfeld & Nicolson, 2014.

Goldsworthy, Adrian. *Caesar.* London: Weidenfeld & Nicolson, 2013.

Goldsworthy, Adrian. *Caesar's Civil War: 49–44 BC.* New York: Routledge, 2013.

Holmes, T. Rice. *Ancient Britain and the Invasions of Julius Caesar.* DigiCat, 2022.

Krebs, Christopher. "More Than Words: The *Commentarii* in Their Propagandistic Context." In *The Cambridge Companion to the Writings of Julius Caesar,* 29–42. Cambridge: Cambridge University Press, 2018.

Montemurro, Nicholas, Alberto Benet, and Michael T. Lawton. "Julius Caesar's Epilepsy: Was It Caused by a Brain Arteriovenous Malformation?" *World Neurosurgery* 84, no. 6 (2015): 1985–1987.

Morrell, Kit. *Pompey, Cato, and the Governance of the Roman Empire.* Oxford: Oxford University Press, 2017.

Morstein-Marx, Robert. *Julius Caesar and the Roman People.* Cambridge: Cambridge University Press, 2021.

Plutarch. *Lives of the Noble Grecians and Romans.* London: Penguin, 1987.

Rosenstein, Nathan, and Robert Morstein-Marx, eds. *A Companion to the Roman Republic.* Malden, MA: Wiley-Blackwell, 2011.

Taylor, Philip M. *Munitions of the Mind: A History of Propaganda from the Ancient World to the Present Era.* Manchester: Manchester University Press, 2013.

Image Sources

1 Portasa Cristian, CC0, via Wikimedia Commons https://commons.
  wikimedia.org/wiki/File:Roman_Republic_and_its_cities_in_100_BC.png

2 https://commons.wikimedia.org/wiki/File:Julius_Caesar_Italian_marble_19th_c..jpg

3 https://commons.wikimedia.org/wiki/File:Sulla_Glyptothek_Munich_309.jpg

4 Mary Harrsch, CC BY-SA 4.0 <https://creativecommons.org/licenses/by-sa/4.0>, via
  Wikimedia Commons, https://commons.wikimedia.org/wiki/File:The_First_
  Triumvirate_of_the_Roman_Republic_720X480.jpg

5 Glauco92, CC BY-SA 3.0 <https://creativecommons.org/licenses/by-sa/3.0>, via
  Wikimedia Commons, https://commons.wikimedia.org/wiki/File:Cicero_-
  _Musei_Capitolini.JPG

6 William Robert Shepherd, CC BY-SA 4.0
  <https://creativecommons.org/licenses/by-sa/4.0>, via Wikimedia Commons;
  https://commons.wikimedia.org/wiki/File:Gaul_in_the_Time_of_Caesar.jpg

7 https://commons.wikimedia.org/wiki/File:Il_ponte_di_Cesare_sul_Reno.jpg

8 https://commons.wikimedia.org/wiki/File:Lionel_Royer_-
  _Vercingetorix_Throwing_down_His_Weapons_at_the_feet_of_Julius_Caesar.jpg

9 Prioryman, CC BY-SA 3.0 <https://creativecommons.org/licenses/by-sa/3.0>, via
  Wikimedia Commons; https://commons.wikimedia.org/wiki/File:
  Cato_Volubilis_bronze_bust.jpg

10 https://commons.wikimedia.org/wiki/File:Battle_of_Pharsalus,_48_BC.png

11 https://commons.wikimedia.org/wiki/File:Kleopatra-VII.-Altes-Museum-Berlin1.jpg

12 https://commons.wikimedia.org/wiki/File:Battle_of_the_Nile_(M._Merian).png

13 George E. Koronaios, CC BY-SA 4.0 <https://creativecommons.org/licenses/by-
   sa/4.0>, via Wikimedia Commons, https://commons.wikimedia.org/wiki/File:

Portrait_of_Julius_Caesar_(1st_cent._B.C.)_at_the_Archaeological_Museum_of_S
parta_on_15_May_2019.jpg

14 Sdwelch1031, CC0, via Wikimedia Commons.
https://commons.wikimedia.org/wiki/File:Caesarion.jpg

15 [1], CC BY-SA 4.0 <https://creativecommons.org/licenses/by-sa/4.0>, via Wikimedia
Commons;
https://commons.wikimedia.org/wiki/File:Battle_of_Munda,_45_BC_(Initial_deplo
yment_of_troops).jpg

16 Ashmolean Museum of Art and Archaeology, CC BY 2.0
<https://creativecommons.org/licenses/by/2.0>, via Wikimedia Commons,
https://commons.wikimedia.org/wiki/File:Roman_coin,_denarius_of_Julius_Caeser
_(FindID_800905).jpg

17 José Luiz Bernardes Ribeiro;
https://commons.wikimedia.org/wiki/File:Forum_of_Julius_Caesar_and_Temple_o
f_Venus_Genitrix_-_Roman_Forums_-_Rome_2016.jpg

18 https://commons.wikimedia.org/wiki/File:Assassination_of_Julius_
Caesar_for_Historia_de_Europa.jpg

19 https://commons.wikimedia.org/wiki/File:Pauwels_Casteels_-
_The_Death_of_Brutus_and_Cassius_at_the_Battle_of_Philippi.jpg

20 Dan Mihai Pitea, CC BY-SA 4.0 <https://creativecommons.org/licenses/by-sa/4.0>,
via Wikimedia Commons; https://commons.wikimedia.org/wiki/File:
Glyptothek_M%C3%BCnchen_%E2%80%93_18.04.2022_%E2%80%93_Augustus
Bevilacqua(4).jpg